1983

D1560248

THE
SUCCESSFUL
YEAR-ROUND
FOOTBALL PROGRAM:

A
Complete
Handbook

Tom Simonton

Parker Publishing Company, Inc. ● West Nyack, New York

Library of Congress Cataloging in Publication Data

Simonton, Tom, 1936–
    The successful year-round football program.

    Includes index.
    1. Football—Coaching. I. Title.
GV956.6.S55   1983   796.332′07′7   82–22385
ISBN 0-13-875559-0

HOW THIS BOOK
CAN HELP ORGANIZE
YOUR FOOTBALL PROGRAM

Football coaching can be divided into two periods. First, there is the *regular* season when so much time must be spent preparing for the games that other football-related duties become burdens. There is also very little time for new ideas during this period. The second phase is the *off-season* when time is more abundant, but lack of sound planning causes a coach to get less than the maximum benefits from his program because he is unsure of what can be done in the off-season. This book helps solve these problems. It not only provides many new ideas to improve your football program, but also provides sample charts for keeping an organized record of general football duties.

The book is divided into twelve chapters, representing months of the year, with each chapter including a list of duties that will improve your football program and serve as a constant reminder that these particular things need to be accomplished immediately.

To use this book, refer to the current month. Here you will find some new ideas that you might not be using with your present team (such as making preliminary off-season scouting reports of each of next fall's opponents). You accomplish this job in the month suggested and make an accurate record that the job has been done.

In some cases there are sample forms that you can duplicate to aid in completing the job. Keep these forms in a file so that quick reference can be made year after year as to how and when you completed the job. By spreading hundreds of jobs related to a successful football program over a period of twelve months you will find that you are not only better organized during the year, but you will have more time for offensive and defensive planning.

Perhaps the best part is this. It is not a book to be read once and placed on the bookshelf. It should be read then placed on your desk so that it can be used daily. At the end of the first year, start over again and use the same organized, systematic outline of the year's football duties. Used properly, this book can save many valuable hours of thought and will insure that no important football job is left unattended.

Tom Simonton

Other Books by the Author

*Coaching the Special Teams: The Winning Edge
    in Football*

*Directory of Surprise Plays for Winning Football:
    How and When to Use Them*

Contents

Chapter 2—FEBRUARY *(cont.)*

Chapter 3—MARCH   44

Chapter 4—APRIL   52

Chapter 4—APRIL *(cont.)*

Chapter 5—MAY   65

Chapter 6—JUNE   78

Chapter 6—JUNE *(cont.)*

Chapter 7—JULY   94

Chapter 8—AUGUST   108

Chapter 8—AUGUST *(cont.)*

Chapter 9—SEPTEMBER   134

Chapter 10—OCTOBER   147

Chapter 12—DECEMBER *(cont.)*

THE
SUCCESSFUL
YEAR-ROUND
FOOTBALL PROGRAM:

A
Complete
Handbook

Make New Varsity Schedule

The making of the varsity football schedule for the coming year (many teams make schedules for a two-year period on a home-and-home basis) will have a solid impact on the success or failure of the team in the fall. The coach must give a great deal of thought to scheduling in order to build a schedule that is both playable and challenging. There are six key points to consider before making the schedule:

1. Do not be intimidated into playing teams that you do not want to play or that you do not think you can compete well with. If you have just completed a bad season, you will undoubtedly receive a lot of phone calls from teams who want to get you on their schedule next fall. Many of these coaches will try to convince you of how weak they are going to be and get your hopes up for an easy victory. Coaches of very strong teams will challenge you to play them saying that the only way to improve is to play championship caliber teams. Regardless of what course you choose to take in your scheduling, just be sure it is in the best interest of your school and players and that you are not talked into playing a schedule you can't handle.

2. Decide whether you want to open the season against strong or weaker opponents. There are two lines of thought on

this. The first is that by playing strong teams early your team will become tougher and better prepared for the lesser teams that you will face later in the season. Other coaches like to take a second approach, that is, they like to open the season with teams they can defeat hoping that this good start will build confidence in the players and enable them to do well the rest of the season. The best solution seems to be this—if you know you've got a good team and your players are used to winning and competing for the league championship it is best to start with tough teams. Even if you lose a game or two early in the season, you will probably rebound and have a winning season and still have a shot at the league title. However, if your team has not done well in the previous seasons you might choose to build a schedule where the first two or three opponents are teams that you have a reasonable chance of defeating. These early wins will build confidence and offer hope for the rest of the season.

3. Separate your key games in your schedule. Determine which games will mean the most to your football program, and build a schedule where these special games are not all played back-to-back. For example, if you must play three tough league opponents plus one key cross-town rival you should try to schedule these games into the 3rd, 5th, 8th, and 10th spots in the schedule rather than playing them *together* in the 2nd, 3rd, 4th, and 5th slots in the schedule.

4. Be aware of home playing dates in your schedule. In a normal ten-game schedule, five of the games should be at home with the other five on the road. Plan so that the home games are spread equally throughout the schedule and are not all bunched up in the first part of the season or the end of the season. The perfect schedule would provide a pattern of *home-away-home-away* games although this is often impossible to work out.

5. Be sure your schedule includes teams that will bring a good following of fans as this will increase your finances at the gate. Schedule teams with football reputations so that fan interest will increase. Schedule teams located near by, not only for the easy travel arrangements, but for the rivalry that most close cities have with each other.

6. The final game of the season should be selected with special care. Many teams like to play their arch-rival in the final game of the season. Even if one team has had a less than productive season, a win in this final game would "make the season a success." Regardless of what team you play in the final game, it is important to win it and end the season on a positive note.

Mimeograph a schedule work sheet like the sample in Figure 1-1. It will help keep track of possible opponents, dates, etc.

SCHEDULE

19___			19___			19___		
Date	Opponent	H-A	Date	Opponent	H-A	Date	Opponent	H-A
___	_____	___	___	_____	___	___	_____	___
___	_____	___	___	_____	___	___	_____	___
___	_____	___	___	_____	___	___	_____	___
___	_____	___	___	_____	___	___	_____	___
___	_____	___	___	_____	___	___	_____	___
___	_____	___	___	_____	___	___	_____	___
___	_____	___	___	_____	___	___	_____	___
___	_____	___	___	_____	___	___	_____	___
___	_____	___	___	_____	___	___	_____	___
___	_____	___	___	_____	___	___	_____	___

Coaches and their phone numbers:

Coach	Team	Phone No.
_____	_____	_____
_____	_____	_____
_____	_____	_____
_____	_____	_____
_____	_____	_____
_____	_____	_____
_____	_____	_____
_____	_____	_____
_____	_____	_____

Figure 1-1

Football Banquet

Tickets: Tickets should be ordered, if not done earlier, and arrangements made to pick them up and distribute them to those in charge of selling them.

Awards: These should have been ordered earlier. Pick them up, carefully check for mistakes such as misspelling of names on trophies.

Guest list: Re-check this list several times to be sure some important name hasn't been omitted. Check the correct pronunciation of hard-to-pronounce names.

Food: Plan last minute menu items. Be sure those in charge give an accurate estimate of the total cost per plate.

Speaker: Contact the previously selected speaker. Double-check times, dates, fee, travel arrangements, plus give details concerning who will meet him, and at what place, on the night of the banquet.

Decorations: See that flowers, etc. have been taken care of and that a committee has been selected to put up *and take down* the decorations.

Programs: Pick up from the printer. Check for errors and get them to the decorating committee.

Microphone: Test well in advance of the banquet to be sure it is working.

Mimeograph the form shown in Figure 1-2 and use it year after year as a final banquet checklist.

Banquet checklist:

	19___	19___	19___	19___	19___	19___
Date set:						
Tickets ready						
Awards ready						
Guests invited						
Meals arranged						
Speaker contacted						
Decorations						
Programs printed						
Microphone						
Other:						
_____						
_____						

Figure 1-2

Two-week Quarterback Indoctrination

If your team has spring practice this two-week quarterback indoctrination course is important. If you do *not* have spring practice, it is even more important!

During this time you should meet daily with all QB prospects to discuss and demonstrate the basic fundamentals of quarterbacking. The head coach, all offensive coaches, plus QB candidates should be present. Pick a time convenient to all. After school seems like the best time, but some may prefer to meet thirty minutes before school or even at night. The candidates should be in shorts or sweats for some sessions. Other sessions may involve blackboard work and not require a change of clothing.

Since you will give the QBs your coaching philosophy at this time of the year, they will have plenty of time to absorb the general pattern of your thinking. By your giving them basic fundamentals, they will have the opportunity to work on their own, and by spring or fall practice they'll be ready to step into more complicated assignments.

Topics such as these could be covered during the two weeks:

- QB leadership and confidence
- General football philosophy of the offensive coaches
- Voice control and cadence
- Taking the snap
- Throwing the football
- Setting up in the pocket
- Footwork and mechanics of executing your basic offensive plays
- Faking
- Handoffs
- Reading defenses
- Weaknesses of different kinds of defenses
- Play calling at different areas of the field (near your own goal, at mid-field, near your opponent's goal, inside opponent's five yard line, etc)
- Ways to save time on the clock
- Ways to keep the clock running
- Calling audibles at the line of scrimmage
- Keeping discipline in the huddle
- Using motion
- Using different offensive sets and formations
- Playing in unusual weather conditions
- Types of blocks that offensive linemen will be using
- Two-minute offense
- Offensive numbering system
- Receiving offensive signals from the coach on the sidelines
- When to use conservative plays
- When to gamble on offense
- Offensive strengths and weaknesses of your own team's personnel
- First, second, third and fourth down play calling

Each coach may wish to expand or reduce this list according to the time available and the experience of his quarterback candidates.

Order Helmets

Many teams have to special-order helmets because local sporting goods companies do not stock large quantities of helmets in a variety of colors. It is best to order these helmets now to insure having them on hand when they are needed. Call your team members together and see who needs a new helmet.

Record your order on a form like the one shown in Figure 1-3.

Helmets:

Year	No. Ordered	Color	Style	Sizes			
19___	_____	_____	____	6¾___	6⅞___	7___	7⅛___
				7¼___	7⅜___	7½___	7⅝___
Company _____				Address _____			
City/State _____ Zip _____				Phone number _____			
Salesman _____							

Figure 1-3

Order Game Pants

Game pants, in your team color, with special stripes down the side, may take three to five months to receive after the order has been placed. By ordering now, you should have the pants at your school before you leave for the summer.

Record your order on a form as shown in Figure 1-4.

Game Pants:

Year	No. Ordered	Color	Stripes	Style	Size
19___	_____	_____	_____		S_M_L_XL_XXL_
Company _____			Address _____		
City/State _____ Zip _____			Phone number _____		
Salesman _____					

Figure 1-4

Order Game Jerseys

Game jerseys usually have to be custom-made at the factory. They will feature your particular colors, sleeve stripes, and number style. They also must be made with the jersey numbers that you want. Before ordering a full set of jerseys make sure the numbers match your other set of jerseys so that you will have matching numbers on both your dark and light set of jerseys (home and away jerseys). If only replacement jerseys are needed, be sure the new jerseys contain the numbers that you need replaced.

Figure 1-5 shows a sample form that you could use to accurately record your order.

Game Jerseys:

Year	No. Ordered	Color	Style	Size	Jersey Numerals Ordered
19__	____	___	___	Small	_____
				Medium	_____
				Large	_____
				X-Large	_____

Company _____ Address _____
City/State _____ Zip ____ Phone number ____
Salesman _____

Figure 1-5

Order Helmet Decals

The reason that decals for the helmets should be ordered now is that many styles have to be custom-made and the entire process of ordering, producing and shipping the decals may take several months. The decals need to arrive before school is out in May (or June) because they may be needed in August (before school actually opens in September).

Figure 1-6 is a sample form to help you record what you ordered and when.

Year	No. Ordered	Style	Color	Name and address of company
19__	____	___	___	_____
19__	____	___	___	_____
19__	____	___	___	_____
19__	____	___	___	_____

Figure 1-6

Check Return of Films from Colleges

No doubt a number of your game films have been sent over the winter to colleges desiring to look at your college prospects in action. By January most of these films should have been checked and returned to you. However, it is easy to misplace game films and a check should be made to insure that all have been returned. A sample form, like the one in Figure 1-7, can help you keep up with your films from year to year.

Check when films have been returned:

Year	1st Opp.	2nd Opp.	3rd Opp.	4th Opp.	5th Opp.	6th Opp.	7th Opp.	8th Opp.	9th Opp.	10th Opp.
19__	__	__	__	__	__	__	__	__	__	__
19__	__	__	__	__	__	__	__	__	__	__
19__	__	__	__	__	__	__	__	__	__	__
19__	__	__	__	__	__	__	__	__	__	__

Figure 1-7

Make Spring Practice Plans

Many high school teams, and most colleges, have spring football practice somewhere between February and April. Serious plans must be made now for that spring practice.

In January the head coach should begin preparing a booklet for each coach to use as a guide through spring practice. A great deal of time should be spent organizing this information so that when spring practice starts each assistant coach will know exactly what is expected of him in the way of drills, offensive and defensive goals, general responsibilities, etc. Following is a sample of the type of coaching booklet we give to each assistant coach at the beginning of spring practice: (Note: we will not attempt to give every word of our booklet here, but rather will give the general information that we try to include.)

Page One gives the table of contents of the booklet, plus the individual coach's name. It also provides important dates concerning spring practice. For example:

19___ Spring Practice Dates:

- Monday, Feb. 4th until Friday, Feb. 15th . . . begin issuing equipment . . . seniors first, then juniors, sophs and, last, freshmen.
- Monday, Feb. 18th . . . start spring practice . . . 3:45 pm
- Friday, March 7th . . . spring game vs. _____ High School
- Friday, March 14th . . . end spring practice
- Tuesday, March 18 . . . Take up equipment and store until fall.

Page Two of the booklet gives coaching assignments.

Sample: Coach _____ ....Quarterbacks and offensive backs
          Coach _____ ....Offensive line
          Coach _____ ....Receivers
          Coach _____ ....Defensive line
          Coach _____ ....Linebackers and safety men
Before and after practice assignments:
          Coach _____ ....Training room
          Coach _____ ....Equipment room
          Coach _____ and _____ ....taping
On-the-field responsibilities:
          Coach _____ ....Have footballs and kicking tees
          Coach _____ ....Lead exercises

Page Three describes the general practice schedule we will follow. Practice schedules are divided into 5-minute periods. A partial practice schedule for the first day might look like this:

Period	Line Coach	Backfield Coach	QB Coach	Receiver Coach
1	Sled	Handoffs	Handoffs	Pass routes
2	Trap blocking	Blocking ends	Passing drill	Downfield block

Page Four is a review of offensive hole numbers, backfield numbers (for play calling), cadence, how to send a back in motion, etc. This should reflect any changes made since the previous fall season.

Page Five reviews each offensive set, and what it is called. Show any new sets (formations) that might be experimented with during the spring.

Page Six lists the basic offensive plays that we will use in the spring plus the formations that we will run each play from. List also any new plays that may be tried.

Page Seven shows a chart taken from game statistics which indicates the most and least successful plays of the past season.

Sample:

Play	Average per carry	Total yards	No. of carrys	TDs	Longest gain
LEAD OPTION	7.7	300	39	2	35
SWEEP	5.6	596	106	6	80
COUNTER	3.1	46	15	0	10

Page Eight gives a review of the passing game, how pass plays are to be called, and the routes to be learned.

Page Nine provides a general review of the defense to be used, including all stunts that will be taught. List also the goal line defense that will be used.

Page Ten gives facts about the special teams, such as:

- Extra points . . . we kicked 25 of 27 with none blocked last fall . . . same kicker returns
- Punting . . . punter graduated . . . was a weak point last fall . . . should improve . . . work with _____ (player's name) who should give us a better punting game
- Snapping . . . probably 90% of our snaps were excellent last fall with the others being good enough to handle . . . top two snappers return
- Punt returns . . . our worst phase of the special teams . . . we did not handle punts well last fall . . . punt return walls were not good . . . we must work long and hard on this

Also on Page Ten indicate which coaches will work directly with which phase of the special teams. (Example: Coach _____ is in charge of snappers. Coach _____ works with kick-off returns.)

Coaches should think all year long about their personnel and which players should play which positions. By January a meeting should be held where the views of each staff member are heard concerning the best position for each player. In many cases players will be tried at two or more positions in spring practice and then a decision will be made as to where to play each in the fall. After the coaches' decisions have been made about spring practice personnel it is a good idea to talk with each player individually and tell him what positions he should learn.

Be sure to take a look at your *football insurance policy*. Some are merely extensions of the fall policy. Other policies may vary in coverage. At any rate make sure each player is covered. Players and parents should be informed of the extent of the policy coverage.

Be sure new players on the football team have had a *physical exam*. Perhaps the team doctor can check these newcomers on a designated day several weeks before spring practice starts.

Make Small Repairs on Uniforms

Check each game jersey, practice jersey, pair of game pants, and practice pants for small tears. Ask the Home Economics class to assist the football program by making the necessary minor repairs to these items. Be sure to supply thread or other materials needed for the repairs. Most tears can be easily repaired and can save the athletic department a great deal of money that otherwise would go to replace these items. It wouldn't hurt public relations to see that the Home Ec. teacher and class members who did the repairs receive a ticket to a future game.

It is a good idea to keep a record of when repairs were made and, in the case of game jerseys and pants, *which* items were repaired (see Figure 1-8).

Year: 19____ Person in charge of repairs: _____
Group making the repairs: _____
Materials supplied to workers: _____
_____
Game jerseys: Color of jerseys: _____
Jerseys with these numerals were repaired: _____
_____
Game pants: Color of pants: _____
Game pants marked with these numbers were repaired: _____
_____
Total number of practice jerseys repaired: _____
Total number of practice pants repaired: _____

Figure 1-8

Two-Week Indoctrination for Receivers

This two-week course for receivers is a good lead in to spring football practice. If your school does not have spring practice, this two-week period can give your receivers plenty to work on and think about during the winter and spring.

All receivers (tight ends, split ends, flankers, slot backs, wing backs) meet with the offensive coaches each day, at a set time and place. Some sessions will involve wearing shorts or sweat clothes. Other meetings will require no change of clothing.

All details and fundamentals of receiving should be taught during this two week period. Since *all* offensive coaches will be working with a limited number of players (possibly 5 to 15 players) personal attention can be given to each player during the day.

Here is a list of items that could be covered:

- Stance
- Releasing off the line
- Downfield blocking
- Receiving drills
- Pass routes
- Faking
- Carrying and protecting the football
- Reading defenses
- Weaknesses of different kinds of defenses
- Adjusting to the quarterback's arm strength (deep routes or short routes)
- Adjusting to audibles
- Going in motion
- Making adjustments for the weather
- Ways to save or use the clock

Each coach may wish to expand or reduce this list according to the time available and the experience of his receivers.

Process College Information or Entrance Papers for Players with Scholarships

By January some members of your team may have received scholarship offers. Work closely with each of these players and the school counselor to advise the player of his course of study and to help him correctly fill out the entrance papers which will be sent to him. Make the player realize the importance of filling out all requests for information *promptly* and to make sure all information is accurate. Make yourself available to the player at all times as requests for information from the college might still be coming in even in early summer. Stress with your players that colleges prefer information typed instead of handwritten, full names instead of nicknames, etc. Before the end of the school year follow up on each of your scholarship players to make certain there are no last minute mix-ups concerning college entrance.

Send College Prospect List of Unsigned Players to Small Colleges

By this time of the year the major colleges have made commitments to the top prospects at your school. But perhaps there are some players on your team who are not major college prospects but certainly have the ability to play small college football. Since many small colleges do not have the recruiting budget to seek out these lesser players it is the responsibility of the high school coach to make the small colleges aware of players with ability. The best way to do this is to mimeograph a sheet containing the player's name, position, size, speed, honors earned, statistics, team record, comments on his character, his grade point average, etc. and send this information along with a short note to each small college in the area. (Be sure the player has some interest in the colleges which are to receive the letters.) The short note should be written personally by the head coach asking the small college recruiter to consider the player. Offer to send game films so the player can be evaluated. It wouldn't hurt to follow the letter with a phone call.

Have Players and Parents Sign Award Jacket Agreement

Occasionally a football player will abuse his award jacket by adding unearned stripes, stars, patches, etc. or perhaps adding his name or nickname to the back of the jacket. If this is a problem at your school you might wish to consider having each award winner, and his parents, sign an *Award Jacket Agreement* as shown in Figure 1-9. Be sure these are kept on file until the player graduates. Also be sure your principal and other top school officials agree with what you are trying to do and will back you up on the agreement. (See page 30.)

Revise Budget Based on New Projected Income

During the preceding summer the athletic department should have made a budget to serve as a guideline for athletic spending. This spending is usually based on the anticipated income from the

AWARD JACKET AGREEMENT

In accepting this letter and jacket from the Athletic Department at
_____ High School I agree to the following terms:

1. I understand that the jacket is the property of _____ High
School Athletic Dept. until I graduate.

2. I am not to add any patches, numbers, letters, stripes, stars,
nicknames, etc. to this jacket unless designated by the head football coach.

3. The jacket will be kept clean and worn with respect at all times.

4. If I should quit the football team (decide not to play anymore), I will return the jacket immediately so that I will not give the impression of being a
varsity football player when I am not. The school will keep the jacket and return it to the owner *when he graduates.* (If a player has to drop football for a
football-related injury, an exception will be made and the player will be allowed to keep the jacket during his school years.)

5. Since I want the wearing of the football jacket to mean something, I
will not allow friends or outsiders to wear the jacket.

I understand and agree with the above terms:

_____   _____
            Player   Parent or guardian

                    _____
                            Date

Figure 1-9

---

revenue sports, mainly football and basketball. Now, in January,
this budget should be examined closely and revisions made if
necessary. This is possible because all the football revenue is in and
one-half of the basketball revenue should also be in. If the seasons
have been successful, and more money taken in than anticipated,
there are three actions that can be taken—(1) put the additional
income in the bank, giving a good start for the following year, (2)
distribute the money to each sport in larger amounts than at first
planned, or (3) purchase "extra" items that might be considered
luxury items such as a new whirlpool, or baseball pitching machine. (The budget is shown on page 31.)

However, *if the mid-year income is less than anticipated*,
budget cuts must be made immediately. Following is an example of
how this can be done. (Note—we will use simplified round figures
so the plan will be easily followed.)

Now, we are in the middle of January and as we look back
over the income so far, we realize that our football gates were not
good due to bad weather at several games, plus having only an
average team. Instead of taking in $27,000 we took in only $20,000.
Halfway through the basketball season we had taken in only $3,000

Budget for 19_____ as developed in August:

Football (equipment, meals, travel, awards,
    banquet, stadium operation, etc.)...$16,000
Basketball (girls' and boys' equipment,
    travel, awards, etc.)...$ 7,000
Baseball ....$ 2,000
Track (girls and boys)..$ 3,000
Tennis (girls and boys)..$ 500
Golf ....$ 500
Cheerleaders (uniforms, travel, etc.) ....$ 500
Wrestling ....$ 1,000

Total budget for school year 19_____ $30,500

Anticipated income for school year 19_____:
Football (5 home games)...$27,000
Basketball (10 home games)...$ 8,000
Total anticipated income..$35,000

---

instead of the $4,000 that we should have taken in by mid season.
Our *new estimate* of income for the school year is now only $26,000
instead of the original $35,000. A check of the total budget shows
we will probably be $4,500 short of what we must have to operate
($30,500). Therefore, cuts must be made. By cutting every sport
20%, football would now have $12,800 to spend (spring practice
would have to suffer here), basketball would have $5600, baseball
now would have $1600, track $2400, tennis $400, golf $400, cheerleaders $400, and wrestling $800. Surely these cuts will hurt, and
coaches will feel they can't make ends meet, but to continue operat-
ing under the *old budget* would end in financial disaster.

Review and Evaluate Game Films

By this time of the year all game films should have been returned from the colleges that were examining them for prospects. Start with the first game film. Spend an entire day or longer analyzing it. Look for and take notes on these things concerning your players, offensive and defensive strategy, execution, etc.:

1. What were our best running plays against this opponent?
2. Which plays should we delete from our offensive plans when we play this team next season?
3. What were our best passing plays against this opponent?
4. Average yards gained from each running and passing play.
5. Outstanding players on our team who will be returning.
6. What is each player's best talent. (Example: can one player block a linebacker better than another? If so, this may determine whether he plays guard or tackle in your offense.)
7. Which players consistently get up quickly after getting knocked down?
8. Count the downfield blocks made on each play. Who makes them? Why are others not making them?
9. Where are we getting hurt on defense, and why?

10. At which *positions* do we have the strongest returning players?
11. Which offensive plays provided the longest runs from scrimmage?
12. Which plays provided the most touchdowns?
13. Who were our most effective special teams players?
14. Which young players played well when they got in the game and what will be each player's best position?

Two-week Indoctrination for Offensive Linemen

Many coaches agree that the offensive line position is one of the most difficult jobs to handle on the entire football team. Linemen have to do plenty of thinking. They must make split-second adjustments. They must know several blocking techniques and when to use each one. This two-week indoctrination can give them a look at the fundamentals they must learn in order for your team to move the football next fall.

First, select your offensive linemen carefully. Look for young players who are willing to learn and who don't mind "not being in the spotlight." Gather them together, along with the offensive coaches, at a time convenient to all. Spend thirty minutes to two hours—as your time permits—going over the basics of offensive line play. Use the blackboard. Sit and talk to them. Take them inside the gym and utilize tumbling mats as you teach techniques and skills. Let them ask questions. Show them the drills that you will be using next fall (or this spring, if you have spring practice).

Be sure to touch on these items:

- Stance
- Firing out
- Making contact
- Maintaining contact
- Drive block
- Reach block
- Reverse shoulder block
- Trap block
- Cutoff block
- Gap block
- Pass blocking (dropback, sprint out, play action)

- Double-team blocking
- Downfield blocking
- Pulling for sweeps
- Blocking the five-man front
- Blocking the six-man front
- Blocking goal line defenses
- Blocking stunting defenses
- Calling blocking assignments at the line of scrimmage

Add other items that your team needs to learn. You'll find that many of your players will continue to practice what they have learned, and will return in the fall better prepared to start the season.

Send Game Contract to Next Fall's Opponents

Most football schedules are set up on a two-year Home-and-Home arrangement, while others might be scheduled for one year only. In either case, a contract showing the teams involved, playing date(s), financial arrangements, and signatures of the coach and at least one school administrator is very important. This is a safeguard against problems and misunderstandings that occur with only verbal commitments. Using a form like the one in Figure 2-1 can help keep up with when contracts were sent out and returned.

	Opponent	Date contract sent	Date returned
1st Game:	_____	_____19___	_____19___
2nd Game:	_____	_____19___	_____19___
3rd Game:	_____	_____19___	_____19___
4th Game:	_____	_____19___	_____19___
5th Game:	_____	_____19___	_____19___
6th Game:	_____	_____19___	_____19___
7th Game:	_____	_____19___	_____19___
8th Game:	_____	_____19___	_____19___
9th Game:	_____	_____19___	_____19___
10th Game:	_____	_____19___	_____19___

Figure 2-1

Figure 2-2 shows a sample contract that can be used by varsity, junior varsity, or lower-level teams.

OFFICIAL CONTRACT—FOOTBALL

_____ High School of _____ (city)
                                          and
_____ High School of _____ (city)
enter into an agreement to play _____ game(s) of football as follows:
                                  (number)

One game will be played at _____(city), _____ (state)
on _____ (date), 19____ .

One game will be played at _____(city), _____ (state)
on _____ (date), 19____.

Players in this game are eligible under the present rules of the State High
School Association.

Financial terms of each game: _____
_____
_____
Officials chosen as follows: _____
_____
_____

Agreed to this _____ day of _____, 19____
School _____   School _____
Superintendent   Superintendent
or   or
Principal_____   Principal_____
AD or Coach _____   AD or Coach _____

Figure 2-2

Make Preliminary Scouting Report
on Next Fall's Opponents

Begin now to gather detailed information on each of next fall's opponents.

1. Review last fall's film of the opponent and note the team's general offensive and defensive _philosophies_ (are they a pass-oriented team or do they prefer to run the ball . . . do they play an attacking defense or do they play a waiting "read" type defense?

2. List opponent's _seniors_ who will graduate, and note their value to the team.

3. Chart opponent's _starters_ on offense and defense who will return.

4. Chart their play tendencies on offense (do they run to their right more than to their left? Do they ever pass on first down inside their own 25 yard line?).

5. What defenses do they use in certain situations?

6. Make notes on what we would do on offense and defense if we were playing them tonight.

7. Secure game films from other teams who have played this opponent. Chart offensive and defensive tendencies which did not appear on your own film.

8. Look for coaching changes (even assistants) that might alter their offensive or defensive plans next fall.

9. Determine if any new players have moved into or out of the opposing school district.

10. Compile all information into a small notebook. Make changes as necessary throughout the spring and summer months.

Plan Junior Varsity and Junior High Schedules

By this time of the year most high schools have completed or nearly completed their varsity schedules for the coming season. Once the varsity schedule is complete, a junior varsity and/or junior high schedule should be arranged. Playing the same schools that the varsity plays is excellent training for these younger players. However, some coaches may prefer to play a tougher schedule with larger schools to better prepare their younger players for future varsity competition. If this is done, be careful not to select teams that will dominate or discourage your younger players. Figure 2-3 illustrates a schedule work sheet that can be helpful as you make calls and finalize your schedules.

Possible games: Use this section for work sheet only.

Junior High			Junior Varsity		
Date	Opponent	Home/Away	Date	Opponent	Home/Away

Possible Opponents:

School	Coach	Phone No.	Address	Comments

Final Schedule:

	Junior High			Junior Varsity	
Date	Opponent	Home/Away	Date	Opponent	Home/Away
_____	_____	_____	_____	_____	_____
_____	_____	_____	_____	_____	_____
_____	_____	_____	_____	_____	_____
_____	_____	_____	_____	_____	_____

Figure 2-3

Select a Football Clinic to Attend This Spring

Most major colleges and many smaller ones provide a clinic in the spring for high school coaches. These clinics provide the high school coach with a chance to visit a college campus, see the facilities, talk with college coaches as well as other high school coaches, and in most cases observe at close range the drills and techniques being taught on the field by the college staff. Care should be taken to choose a college whose offensive and defensive philosophies blend well with what you plan to teach.

Some coaches prefer to contact a college and ask permission to visit for several days during the spring, but not during the regular clinic week. They feel that they will have more freedom to talk with the college staff if there are not many other coaches around. If this method is chosen, a letter should be sent well in advance of the desired date requesting permission to come.

Usually in February or March, colleges will send brochures to high school coaches in the area indicating the details of their clinics. Save these brochures or use a form similar to the one in Figure 2-4 to compare information and select the best clinic for you and your staff.

College: _____ _____ _____
Clinic dates: _____ _____ _____
Head coach: _____ _____ _____
Main speakers: _____ _____ _____

Other features: _____ _____ _____
_____ _____ _____

Cost of clinic: _____ _____ _____
Transportation: _____ _____ _____
Motel/Housing _____ _____ _____
Comments: _____ _____ _____
_____ _____ _____

Figure 2-4

Check Players' Grades and Talk with Teachers

Now is a good time to find out which players may be having grade problems. Since there are at least three months left in the year there is still time to improve the grades of any player having trouble.

First, have each player fill out a card showing his schedule, teacher's name, room number, and period. Plan a visit to each teacher at the teacher's convenience. Have ready a list of all players taught by this teacher (see Figure 2-5)

Grade Check Sheet:
Teacher ————————————— Room Number —————————

Player	Present Grade	Conduct	Comments

Figure 2-5

Present the list to the teacher asking for comments both good and bad. Ask the teacher for suggestions for improving the work of players who are doing poorly.

After all grades and comments are completed, meet with those players who need help. Warn them of their low grades and what it can mean to their football futures at your school. In a few weeks do a follow-up comparison of grades to see if low grades have been brought up to standards.

Two-Week Indoctrination for Defensive Linemen

Regardless of whether there is a spring practice or not it is good to get specialized groups of players together during the off-season. This group involves all defensive linemen, their coaches, plus the head coach. After finding a convenient time to meet (usually for thirty minutes to two hours each day) begin teaching the players the skills they need to master to become efficient defensive players. There may be only six or eight players to work with, or you may be looking at over twenty linemen. Whatever the number, use varied methods to teach the fundamentals of defensive line play so that next fall they will start the season knowing what is expected of them. Some coaches will want to keep this two-week period very informal, with plenty of time for players to stop, ask questions, and review what they are learning. Here are some of the things that can be taught and worked on during the two week indoctrination period:

- Stance
- Forearm lift
- Hand shiver
- Form tackling
- Pursuit angles
- Rushing the passer
- Reading the screen pass
- Reading the draw play
- Playing the trap block
- Fighting pressure
- Basic techniques of playing your particular type of defense
- Techniques of playing goalline defense

During this two-week indoctrination period, players should wear shorts, T-shirts, sweat clothes, tennis shoes, etc. Be sure to use the gym during bad weather. Also use the chalkboard for teaching and explaining your defense and its philosophy. Keep in mind that while this is only an off-season learning experience, it can enable you to start next fall at a more advanced pace.

Send Football Schedule to All Band, Touchdown Club, Cheerleader, etc. Groups

There are plenty of people who, like the football coach, need to determine as early as possible the dates and opponents for next fall's season. Travel plans, homecoming activities, school dances, etc. will be built around the football schedule. Businessmen and other townspeople will often make their schedules to avoid conflict with local games.

As soon as the season's schedule is complete have copies mimeographed or printed and distribute them to all school supporters. Have different size schedules available ranging from large poster type schedules for bulletin boards or store windows, to small billfold size schedules. Giving out schedules now will save many inquiries later when the coach is busy with other things. It is a good public relations move and will keep your team in the public eye. Figure 2-6 shows a chart that can be used to keep track of when schedules were given out and to whom.

Group	Date given out	Size	Number	Person receiving schedules
TD Club				
Band				
Cheerleaders				
Pep Club				
Superintendent				
Principal				

List others (banks, radio and TV stations, newspapers, stores, etc.):

Figure 2-6

Select Game Officials for Next Fall

In many cases this will be a simple process of contacting the association of officials that worked your games last fall. However, if those officials were unsatisfactory, it is certainly your privilege to talk with other associations. Although most associations are basically the same, some are more organized than others. For example, some associations send a list of officials scheduled to work your game several days in advance of the game. This is helpful.

Remember, the officials need you as much as you need them. Contact several associations in your area and ask each to come by your office for a visit. Request that they bring a list of their officials and the number of years experience each has. After talking with each group, sign a contract with the association you feel most comfortable with. A chart like the one shown in Figure 2-7 will help you compare associations and make a choice.

Sign Contract with Officials Association

Once you have chosen an association of officials for next fall make sure a contract is signed. Usually the association will provide the contract. If they don't, you supply one. By all means don't

Name of Association: _____ _____ _____
President: _____ _____ _____
Address: _____ _____ _____
Phone: _____ _____ _____
Cost per official: $_____ $_____ $_____
No. of registered
officials: _____ _____ _____
Comments: _____ _____ _____
_____ _____ _____

Figure 2-7

leave this vital matter unattended or you may end up with two
teams, a group of fans, and no officials at game time. Figure 2-8
illustrates a sample football official's contract.

FOOTBALL OFFICIAL'S CONTRACT

The _____(name of association)
Football Official's Association agrees to supply officials to
_____ High School of _____ (city) for the 19____
football season. All officials must be approved by the state officials association and be in good standing. Schedule of games to be officiated:

Home team	Opponent	Site	Date	Game time	No. of Officials
_____	_____	_____	_____	_____	_____
_____	_____	_____	_____	_____	_____
_____	_____	_____	_____	_____	_____
_____	_____	_____	_____	_____	_____

Fee per official will be: $_____
Agreed to this date: _____ 19____
_____ High School _____ Association
_____ Principal _____ Signed
_____ AD or Coach _____ Title

Figure 2-8

Send Projector for Repairs

As soon as work has been completed on your films and films of
future opponents, the projector should be sent to a reliable repair
shop. This allows the projector to be gone during the part of the
school year when the demand for film work is not heavy. Also, by
being sent now the projector is sure to be back before the end of
the school year and will be ready for summer work before practice
starts in August.

It is a good point to remind the repair shop to correct any

potential trouble spot now. Once the season starts, the projector will be in constant use and you will not have time to make repairs. Also, be sure to purchase several extra light bulbs to have on hand when the one in use burns out. A chart like the one in Figure 2-9 will help you keep an accurate record from year to year about when and where you sent the projector for repairs.

	19___	19___	19___
Date sent for repairs:	_____	_____	_____
Name of repair company:	_____	_____	_____
Address:	_____	_____	_____
City/State:	_____	_____	_____
Zip:	_____	_____	_____
Phone No.:	_____	_____	_____
Date returned:	_____	_____	_____
Cost:	$_____	$_____	$_____
List repairs that were made:	_____	_____	_____

Figure 2-9

Begin Spring Practice

(*Note:* Many high schools are located in states where spring practice is not allowed. However, if it *is* allowed in your area, this part of the book should provide an adequate checklist of things to do before starting.)

Check Player's Names on Insurance List—Be sure that all players taking part in spring drills have insurance coverage as they do in the fall during the regular season. Read last fall's policy carefully to see if spring practice players are covered. If not, take steps to provide coverage for each team member. *Never* allow an uninsured person to participate in practice of any kind until adequate coverage is provided.

Provide Spring Practice Physical Exam—For those who played in the fall this might not be needed. However, be sure to check any player who had a serious injury in the fall to be sure he is ready to resume practice. For those who haven't had a physical exam within the school year, an exam by a local physician is necessary. Call a team doctor and set up a date to examine these new players. By all means never let a person play without a physical exam. This is for the protection of the boy first, and for the coach and school as well.

Secure Pads on Blocking Sleds—Do not wait until the last minute to do this seemingly minor task. Be sure the straps and buckles are strong and tight.

Check Medical Kit for all Necessary Supplies—At least a week before the start of practice, review the contents of the medical kit. Be sure it is clean and filled with all necessary on-the-field supplies. Review the list of medical supplies shown in Chapter Eight (August).

Check Footballs, Scrimmage Vests, and Extra-point Tees—Pump up the footballs. Place scrimmage vests in a bag that can be easily carried on the field. Provide enough kicking tees for your kicking specialists. Chalkboards, chalk, etc. may also be wanted on the field.

Line Field—A marked field provides for better practices. Some may wish to line a 100 yard field. Others may prefer only a 50 yard area.

Issue Equipment—Do this at least one week before the start of practice. This allows the final week for individual adjustments.

Review Manager's Duties—If your managers are holdovers from last fall, review their duties with them. Instruct new managers on what you expect from them.

Plan for Spring Game—If you hold any type of spring game at the conclusion of spring drills be sure you have provided for these things: game officials, film crew, chain holders, team doctors, concession stand operations, media coverage, ticket takers, security, a check of stadium lights, a check of the scoreboard and P.A. system.

(Depending on your location in the country, spring practice might be held any time from February to May.)

Conclude Spring Practice

(*Note:* Schools in some states are not allowed to conduct a spring practice. However, the following notes should be helpful for those who do have spring football drills.)

The chapter for February gives some ideas for organizing and beginning spring football practice. Here are some reminders of things that need to be done at the *end* of spring practice:

Conclude Spring Practice with a Spring Game—Some states allow their schools to end spring drills with a regular game with another school. This is an excellent opportunity to see your players under actual game conditions where they must make adjustments, read defenses, and use all the other skills they have worked to learn. If you are not allowed to play against another school, perhaps a game against your graduating seniors or an intrasquad scrimmage will add excitement to the end of spring drills.

Recount, Clean, and Store Game Uniforms—If game uniforms were used for a spring game of any type, be sure they are cleaned and properly stored for the next few months until the regular season begins.

File Injury Claims for Those Injured During Spring Drills—Be sure all players who were injured have filled out the proper insurance claim papers and that these have been mailed to the insurance company. It is your job, as the coach, to see that the insurance company has paid full benefits to the player and that the player's family is satisfied with the handling of the claim.

Store Dummies, Sled Pads, Chains, and Down Marker—Be sure to clean these items, especially the sled pads and dummies before storing them.

Clean and Organize Equipment Room and Medical Room—First, take everything out of the room. Then clean the room throughly and place each item of equipment or medical supply back in the room in good order ready for use in the fall. Be sure to throw away any medical supplies that should not be used again.

Secure the Stadium Gates, Press Box and Ticket Booths—If the stadium was used for the spring game or for any practice sessions, be sure it is locked up. Before doing this, clean the stadium so that it is ready for fall use.

Review Fall Equipment Needs Based on Wear and Tear of Spring Practice—Compare the available usable equipment with the projected needs for the fall to determine if new equipment must be ordered.

Two-week Linebacker Indoctrination

If no spring practice was held, this is a good time to begin work with next fall's linebackers. Regardless of the type defense a coach chooses to use, the selection and training of his linebackers will go a long way in determining how successful the defense will be.

Have your linebackers dress in shorts, sweats, tennis shoes, etc. and meet daily with the defensive coaches. The time allotted for these meetings may vary, but should be a minimum of thirty minutes. Meetings may be held in the morning before school, in the afternoon, or even at night. The purpose of the meetings is to give the linebackers some advanced work connected with the defense to be used in the fall. Fundamentals should be taught, drills explained, and strategy discussed so that when the players return to practice in the fall they will not waste time by having the basics of the defense explained for the first time. This two-week period also gives the defensive coaches an opportunity to look over the talent that is available. This will aid in determining which players are the fastest, the strongest, etc. Some fundamentals that can be stressed are these:

- Stance
- Reading the blocker
- Using the forearm
- Pursuit angles
- Form tackling
- Sideline tackling

- Reading the screen
- Reading the draw play
- Playing pass defense
- Stunting
- Goal line defense
- Calling defensive signals

Film Offensive and Defensive Techniques for Training Film

One of the best ways to teach offensive plays and defensive stunts and movements is to record your techniques on film exactly as you want them to be executed. All you need will be your camera, your cameraman, several hundred feet of 16mm film, your top 11 offensive players and your top 11 defensive players. Start by dressing the offensive players in dark jerseys and the defensive players in light jerseys. On the field explain exactly which offensive play you want run, exactly how to block it, and how you want the defense to react. Then run through it live as the cameraman films the play. After finishing your offensive sets and plays, film the defense moving through their stunts, adjustments, etc. It is usually a good idea to use last fall's top football players in the film as they have the experience to run the plays properly and will know exactly how you want them run.

This film will provide an excellent teaching guide for years to come as you show it in slow motion pointing out time and again the correct way to execute each movement. Save the film and add to it year after year as your plays and techniques change.

Repair or Reorder All Field Markers

Do not save this until fall because it can cause a lot of last-minute problems on the day of the game. Field markers (rubber or plastic markers with 20, 30, etc. yard line indicated on them) often take a beating during the season as players fall on and roll over them. Be sure the markers are in good condition. Some may need repainting. Others may not "stand up" properly where they can be seen. Once these are in good shape, store them in the equipment room ready for fall use.

Counsel Players on Selecting Spring Sports

After playing football in the fall and basketball or wrestling in the winter, some football players may plan to take the spring season off. In many cases this may be good. The football coach should meet with each player to help him determine his spring plans. An athlete with speed should be encouraged to run track which will not only help the track team, but will help increase the player's speed for football. Athletes hoping for a football scholarship might find their athletic ability will be noticed and their name in the newspaper more by excelling in a spring sport. Some players who need to keep their weight down might be encouraged to take part in some spring sport. The main idea, however, is for the football coach to know exactly what each player is doing to improve himself as an athlete.

Select Homecoming Game for Fall

March is a good month for making a selection of the Homecoming game for next fall because there are so many people who may be involved and many plans have to be made early. Homecoming activities such as dances, parades, etc. need to be planned far in advance. Committees need to be set up to select candidates for Homecoming Queen. Most people connected with Homecoming would appreciate knowing at this early point in the year the first choice of dates plus an alternate date. In selecting a Homecoming date keep these points in mind:

Never select the *opening* home game. A good crowd should be on hand for this game regardless of what other activities you have planned (Homecoming tends to draw a large crowd). Also there is not time to select the Queen, etc.

Never select the *last* game of the schedule. This leaves no alternate date in case of bad weather.

Of the two or three mid-season home games, select the game where there will be the fewest visiting fans. The home crowd, wanting to see the Homecoming activities should be large enough to keep gate receipts at a normal level despite the absence of visiting fans.

If possible select a game you have a good chance of winning. Homecoming isn't much fun when you lose.

Once the date has been set, be sure to inform the school administration, the cheerleaders, the band, the Touchdown Club, and any other organization that might be involved. Also get the date in the newspaper and on the radio so that people not related with the school can avoid picking that date for other community affairs.

Two-week Indoctrination for Defensive Safetymen

If there has been no spring practice the defensive coaches should gather their potential defensive backs for informal sessions relating to playing the secondary. All coaches who have anything to do with the defensive planning should be present. Players should wear shorts or sweats according to the weather. Some sessions might be in the gym while others could be outside or in a classroom using the blackboard. Have about ten sessions (five per week) teaching fundamentals of secondary play. The more that is taught now, the better prepared the players will be in the fall. Give the players ample time to ask questions and not be rushed (as they might be in the fall with the busy game week schedule). Some things that can be discussed and practiced are these:

- Stance
- Backward running
- Tip drills
- Catching ball at its height
- Form tackling
- Sideline tackling
- Pursuit angles
- Reading offensive linemen
- Coming up fast on sweeps
- Man-to-man techniques
- Zone techniques
- Adjusting to split ends, flankers, etc.
- General philosophy of your style defense

Coaches' Meeting to Determine Offense to Be Used in Fall

By this time of the year all coaches have had time to reflect for several months on the past season. Films have been viewed and reviewed. Coaches have talked informally about returning players.

Spring practice (if allowed) has been concluded. It is time to meet with all coaches concerning offensive plans for the fall.

Set a time convenient to all, perhaps an evening or during the weekend, when no one will feel rushed. You need time to discuss the pros and cons of using certain offensive sets, running plays and pass routes. You must match your offense to the talents of your players. Encourage all coaches to contribute ideas and suggestions. You may wish to follow this agenda:

1. Start by listing the name of each player expected out for football next fall. As each name is read, all coaches should comment on the best position for that player. List the player at that position on the chalkboard so all can see. If the player has another position on offense which he might also play, list him at the bottom of that position's list. (This can be useful later—for example, the name David Norwood may appear at the top of the QB list and at the bottom of the split end list. There may be another capable QB but no other capable split ends. The listing on the chalkboard will show that Norwood is needed more at split end.)

2. Once all the players have been listed look at their talents and determine the type offense best for your team. Power offense? Passing offense? Offense based on speed?

3. Once the offensive style (I formation, Veer, etc.) has been determined, begin selecting plays from that formation *that can be executed by the type of players you have.* Be sure to include all types of plays—traps, sweeps, counters, dives, etc.

4. Determine your passing style—dropback, play action, or sprint out. Decide on the best type passes for *your* talent—short passes, long passes, passes to backs coming out of the backfield, etc.

5. Now take a good look at what you have come up with. Are you satisfied with your offensive plans? Do you think you can win with the things you have decided to do? If so, carefully write everything down (offensive sets, plays, snap count, etc). Within the next few days neatly mimeograph the material and present it in booklet form to every staff member.

Request Money for Football Clinic

Last month's chapter suggested selecting a football clinic to attend this spring. Money will be needed for travel, motels, food, and possibly a clinic fee. Touchdown clubs often supply enough money to send the staff to one clinic each year. If the school athletic budget is in good shape, this is a good source of revenue. Be sure to request the money well in advance so that Touchdown Club members or school officials (depending on where the money comes from) can consider the expense and have the money available when needed. Remember that some clinics require a clinic fee sent *in advance*.

Coaches' Meeting to Determine Offensive Drills to Be Used in the Fall

Once the offense for the fall has been designed (see page 48 in this chapter) all coaches should meet to determine what type drills will be used to best teach the offense. Look carefully at each offensive play. Review each offensive position and determine what skill is needed to execute the play. For example, on one play the tight end might need to use a double-team block with the tackle. The left guard might need to pull and lead the play while the center executes the cutoff block. Do this for each offensive play and each position on the team. Then compile the lists to determine all the skills each position must learn. All coaches should now contribute ideas concerning the best drills to use to teach the techniques needed to execute the offense. Make a careful list of these drills, mimeograph them and distribute them to all offensive coaches.

Return to Off-season Conditioning Program (if spring practice was held)

Once spring practice has been completed all players who completed spring drills with the varsity or junior varsity (B team) should begin working with the off-season program. *Important: Refer to the December chapter of this book which describes how to set up the off-season program.* There are many different ideas among coaches concerning what to expect of football players after spring practice. Some prefer to free the players entirely, allowing them to play spring sports or pick up part-time jobs. Other coaches require those players who are not engaged in school-related sports to get involved with the off-season program. A few coaches require *all* players, regardless of other activities, to take part in off-season drills. Each coach must decide which plan best suits his school situation and personal preference. However, *if* an off-season program is held for the spring months, now is the time to start it.

Alter Off-season Conditioning Program to Include Basketball Players as They Finish Their Season, and Release Spring Sports Athletes

(*Note: this section applies mainly to schools that do not have spring football practice.*) As soon as basketball season is over, those athletes who also play football should be worked back into the football off-season conditioning program. Keep in mind that many of these players will need instruction in the type of weights they should begin with, how much running they should do, etc. (Other players received this instruction in December when the program started.) Also remember that the basketball-playing athletes should not be expected to start their workouts at the same level as those football players who began in December.

While some (basketball players) are joining the off-season program, others will be leaving during this month of March. Those who play baseball, tennis, golf, and run track should begin practicing these sports. Before they leave you may wish to test these athletes to see how they have improved themselves since the beginning of the program. Also counsel them on when you expect them to return to the football off-season program (usually after the spring sport season, or perhaps at the beginning of the summer.)

Talk with Each Coach Concerning Contract and Football Duties for Next Fall

April is an excellent time for the head coach to sit down with each member of his staff individually and talk frankly about the assistant coach's football future. Encourage the assistant coach to open up and express his feelings so that a clear understanding between head coach and assistant exists concerning all football matters.

Points for discussion:

1. Review the past fall's season in relation to the strong and weak points shown by the assistant. Be careful not to criticize, but offer suggestions as to the areas where the assistant can work to improve. Talk about how the assistant can be utilized better during practice and during games. Allow the assistant an opportunity to make suggestions concerning practice schedules, offensive plans, defensive plans, etc.

2. Talk with the assistant about his off-season football duties and get ideas to improve the off-season conditioning program.

3. Review the assistant's public relations work. Did he talk up the football program at every opportunity?

4. Evaluate the spring practice (if this was held) of the assistant. Did he seem to improve in his knowledge of football or does

he seem content to do his work the same way time and again even if the results aren't successful.

5. Evaluate how the assistant gets along with others on the staff. If he is in conflict with others, find out what the problem is and work toward a solution.

6. Talk with the assistant about his plans for the future. Is he looking for a head job on his own? Is he considering leaving for another assistant's job? What new duties would he like assigned to him?

A winning season starts with an excellent staff. Be sure your people are loyal and dedicated to your program. Talks such as those described here should do much to improve staff relations.

Complete and Distribute Junior Varsity and Junior High Schedules

In February (see Chapter 2) you were advised to start making schedules for all teams under the varsity level. Hopefully this has been completed. There are three points to keep in mind:

1. Be sure to complete the schedule with the maximum number of games allowed. (Be sure not to go over the allowed number of games. Some states allow junior varsity teams to play 80% of the number of games the varsity plays, with the junior highs playing about 60%).

2. Double-check these games and dates with all schools especially if any school has hired a new head football coach who might not be aware of lower level games that have been scheduled.

3. Send copies of junior varsity and junior high schedules to all school administrators, cheerleader sponsors, band people, newspaper and radio/TV stations. The only way to create interest in your younger program is to publicize it.

If there is a team pending on the schedule but dates and details are not complete, it would be a good idea to get home telephone numbers of those you are in contact with, so that calls can be made throughout the summer concerning the schedule.

Two-week Indoctrination for Punters and Snappers

If no spring practice was held you may wish to take some time to work exclusively with punters and snappers. Issue a call to all potential varsity punters or snappers to begin a two-week instructional period. Utilize all coaches or at least those most directly concerned with the kicking game. Work outside when possible as the weather should be good this time of the year. If you must work inside there are plenty of drills and instruction that can be taught. Practice may be after school or perhaps at night if several of the punters/snappers are playing baseball or running track. Spend ten practice periods (five per week) working on fundamentals of the punting game. Examples of things to work on:

Punters	Snappers
Receiving the snap	Gripping the ball
Rotating the ball in your hands	Checking blocking assignments
Dropping the football	Snapping to the punter
Proper kicking foot techniques	Blocking after the snap
Follow-through	Releasing from the line
Kicking out of bounds	Covering the punt
Kicking dead inside the 10 yard line	Breaking down before the tackle
Covering the punt	Snapping a wet football
Punting a wet football	
Proper distance to align from the snapper	
Handling a low/high snap	
Running or passing the football if bad snap makes no punt possible	
Punting from the end zone	

Make Plans to Fertilize and Plant Seed on Game and Practice Fields

Practice and game fields have gone through fall (and perhaps spring) practice and now attention must be given to preparing them for the coming fall season. If the coach is not knowledgable about field and stadium upkeep, he should consult school grounds personnel or local citizens for advice. A chart such as the one shown in Figure 4-1 will help keep an accurate record of when fields were prepared.

Coaches' Meeting to Determine Defensive Plans for the Fall

By April your staff should be making some pretty definite plans for your fall defense. There has been plenty of time to discuss the pros and cons of your defensive efforts of last season. In some

	Practice Field		Stadium	
	Mo/date/Yr.	Notes	Mo/Date/Yr.	Notes
Fertilize:	__/__/__	_____	__/__/__	_____
		_____		_____
		_____		_____
	__/__/__	_____	__/__/__	_____
		_____		_____
	__/__/__	_____	__/__/__	_____
		_____		_____
		_____		_____
Plant Seed:	__/__/__	_____	__/__/__	_____
		_____		_____
		_____		_____
	__/__/__	_____	__/__/__	_____
		_____		_____
	__/__/__	_____	__/__/__	_____
		_____		_____
		_____		_____

Type of fertilizer used: _____

Type of seed planted: _____

_____

Figure 4-1

cases, spring practice has been held. Perhaps two-week indoctrination courses have been held for all defensive personnel (see Chapters 2 and 3).

Start by gathering all staff members for an afternoon or night meeting. Set no time limit so that no one will feel rushed to make decisions.

Look first at the defensive personnel you will have to work with. Select from your roster of players those capable of playing defense (some players are offensive specialists or kickers). List the names of these people on a chalkboard. Study the list to see where your strengths and weaknesses lie. Are you big? Are you quick and fast? Do you have experience? How does this fall's talent compare with last season's talent?

Now decide if you are still capable of using last season's defense with the talent you now have. Discuss what changes in the defense you might need to make. Consider alternate defenses that might better suit next fall's personnel.

After you have decided on the defense(s) to be used, go over the techniques of playing the defense in detail. Be sure all are in agreement as to how to coach the techniques, make adjustments to different offensive sets, etc. Later, compile all information, mimeograph and distribute it to all staff members.

Paint Helmets

By April several decisions concerning helmets should have been made: (1) How many new helmets will be purchased? (2) How many used helmets are in good condition? (3) How many players are expected on the team in the fall? (4) Will there be any change in color or style of helmets?

After these questions have been answered gather all the helmets that need painting. Secure the proper type of paint. Avoid paint that is easy to chip or flake. Spread a large canvas or cloth on the floor, or perhaps, outside. Take the face mask or bar off the helmet, being careful not to misplace the hardware (screws, etc). Spray the helmets evenly. Some will prefer to paint the face mask also. Add a second coat later. Allow time to dry completely and replace facemasks and bars. (Note: face masks and bars should be labeled to insure replacing the proper mask or bar on the proper helmet.)

Two-week Indoctrination for Extra-Point, Field-Goal and Kick-off Men

Regardless of whether your team had a spring practice, it is a good policy to spend special time with extra-point, field-goal, and kick-off personnel. Few players can be as valuable to the success or failure of your team as these people.

Gather all your kicking coaches (or the entire staff if possible). Invite all potential kickers to meet each day (or night) for two weeks. Always work outside if weather permits. You may also wish to have snappers (and EP holders) work with the kickers. In addition to on-the-field teaching have several sessions where players and coaches discuss strategy. For example; in what situations you will probably go for two points rather than kick an extra point . . . what to do if the holder for a field goal gets a bad snap . . . or how to avoid kicking off to the opponent's top return man (kick to opposite side, or kick short).

End the two-week session by setting kicking goals for your

players. Also instruct them on what they should do (on their own) during the summer months to improve. Be sure to provide each kicker with one or several footballs, kicking tees, etc.

Water Practice Field and Stadium Grass

After the fertilization and planting of seed (see page 54 in this chapter) has been completed a definite plan should be set up to supply ample water for the fields. Unlike being at home, you won't be at school (practice field and stadium) every time water is needed. Keep a simple chart (see Figure 4-2) to help remember how often both fields have been watered. It is a good idea to notify school administrators and other coaches concerning your water schedule. Perhaps other coaches and student managers will alternate watering the fields so that the burden won't rest on the head coach.

Date watered: Comments:
Practice field _____ Stadium _____ _____

Figure 4-2

Under the "comments" section make notes such as "has rained all week, no extra water needed," or perhaps write the names of those responsible for watering the fields that particular week.

Coaches' Meeting to Determine Defensive Drills to Be Used in the Fall

Earlier in this chapter it was suggested that defensive coaches meet and decide defensive personnel and type of defense to be used. Once that has been completed, coaches should meet again to determine the best drills to use to teach the defensive techniques. Utilize the thoughts of all coaches plus any football books which contains drills. Make a master list of all drills that would help teach your defense. Then mimeograph a list for each defensive coach. Encourage your coaches to watch constantly for new drills to add to the list.

Evaluate Several Football Insurance Plans and
Select a Policy for the Fall

Contact any insurance companies that deal with high school football insurance and ask them to send a representative to see you about a football insurance policy for next season's football players. Listen carefully to each company explain its benefits. It is a good idea to have your school principal or business manager in on the meeting. Decide what you want in your policy. Determine how much money you will have available for insurance. Here are some points to consider:

1. Were you satisfied with last season's policy?
2. Did last season's policy pay promptly?
3. Did they pay all that you thought they would?
4. Were the parents pleased with the service the company rendered?
5. Do you want your policy to cover spring practice?
6. Do you want the same policy to cover junior varsity players?
7. How much paper work is involved with filing a claim?
8. Are you dealing with a well-known company?
9. Do any other schools in the area use the same company that you are considering? Were they pleased?
10. Is there a representative living near by so that personal attention can be given to your school's needs?
11. Will the players or the school, or both, finance the insurance policy?

Figure 4-3 is a sample work sheet to help you keep up with companies you have used in the past or might consider in the future.

Have Players Fill Out Equipment Size Cards

A great deal of time can be saved next fall when equipment is given out if the coaches have an idea of the sizes that will be needed. This will also help in ordering any equipment in the future.

Use the card in the late summer to select each player's equipment and place it in front of his locker, ready to go when he reports in the fall. Then, if a player has outgrown something you

School Year—19____
Name of Company: _____
Address: _____
Phone: _____ Name of Representative: _____
Notes: _____
_____

School Year—19____
Name of Company: _____
Address: _____
Phone: _____ Name of Representative: _____
Notes: _____
_____

School Year—19____
Name of Company: _____
Address: _____
Phone: _____ Name of Representative: _____
Notes: _____
_____

School Year—19____
Name of Company: _____
Address: _____
Phone: _____ Name of Representative: _____
Notes: _____
_____

Figure 4-3

have given him, it will be a simple matter of exchanging that *one* piece of equipment. (Note: when this happens, be sure to change the size on the player's card.)

Here is a sample *Equipment Size Card* (Figure 4-4). Have a team meeting and let each player fill out his card. You may even want him to take it home so his parents can help him with some of the sizes.

Player's Name _____School _____
Grade _____ Coach _____Date _____
Player's Age _____ Birthday _____Phone _____
Ht. _____ feet, _____ inches   Wt. _____ lbs.
Helmet size: _____ Shoulder Pads: sm.__ med.__ lg.__
Jersey size: sm.__ med.__ lg.__ X-lg.__
Pants size: 26__ 28__ 30__ 32__ 34__ 36__ 38__ 40__ 42__
Hip pads: sm.__ med.__ lg.__ X-lg.__
Shoe size: _____
Other: _____

Figure 4-4

Attend a Football Clinic

In Chapter 2 it was suggested that you select a football clinic to attend, and in Chapter 3 money was hopefully found to help with clinic expenses. Here are some things to keep in mind as you attend the clinic.

1. Be sure to have your classes covered if you must miss school.
2. Carry as many assistant coaches as you feel can benefit from the clinic.
3. Look over the clinic meeting schedule and select those lectures and demonstrations which will mean most to your football program. For example, if you feel your team's weakness is the passing offense spend as much time as possible with those coaches (or clinic lecturers) who specialize in the passing game.
4. Don't feel as though you must write down every word said, but do keep notes on items, drills, plays, etc. that you are especially interested in.
5. Don't be afraid to approach other coaches or lecturers and ask specific questions. All coaches are eager to talk football and will be glad to help you. In some cases films might be available so that you can study techniques of blocking, running pass routes, etc.
6. When you return home, write down those things you learned that were most beneficial. Share them with those coaches who were unable to attend the clinic.

Splice Highlight Film of Previous Season's Games

Some coaches will not look favorably upon cutting up their game films just to make a highlight film. We were among the greatest doubters . . . until we finally decided to do it. Now we wouldn't be without a highlight film. Follow these steps to create your highlight film:

1. Starting with your first game of the season, review each game film. Run the film through until you come to a *highlight* play. This can be a touchdown, a long run, a long pass, a key field goal, a long well-covered punt or kick-off, or a great defensive play such as a quarterback sack, an interception, or key fumble recovery.

2. Using a *splicing machine* cut away the highlight play then splice the film back together (this is important because the basic remaining film will serve as a scouting film when you play this opponent this fall.)

3. Splice all the highlight clips together in order from the first game to the final game of the season. Some coaches may prefer to place all long runs back-to-back, then all pass interceptions back-to-back, etc. (this would make a good teaching guide for future players as they work on certain aspects of the game such as pass defense).

4. Be sure to add some lead in (blank) film at the beginning as well as at the end to make the showing of the film smoother.

There are many uses for the highlight film:

1. Show it at the conclusion of a football banquet.

2. Show it next fall, before taking the field for your first game (as a motivational instrument).

3. Use it to help interest young players at your school in your football program.

4. Make it available to any civic clubs in town for showing at one of their meetings.

5. Take it to your feeder elementary schools or junior high schools to interest younger boys in your program.

6. Make it available to college recruiters as they look for prospects.

7. Use it as a teaching guide (most of these highlight plays are well executed and can illustrate "how the play should look if run properly".

Visit Feeder Elementary Schools and
Make Contact with Future Players

There are a number of elementary schools in your area that will feed potential football players into your junior high football program. Now is a good time to visit these students and encourage them to join your lower grade football program.

Start by contacting the principal of the school that you plan to visit. Ask for a few minutes at the end of a day. Keep in mind that the principal and teachers will not be willing to have too much of their class time taken away by your visit.

Once the potential players are seated introduce yourself and your staff. Briefly state the purpose of your visit—the hope that each boy will join your junior high program in the fall. Tell them a little about the schedule that they will play and something about their coaches. Explain exactly what equipment will be furnished to them. Talk about the starting date of practice in the fall (or late summer). It is important that you give each boy a mimeographed copy of a letter to his parents reviewing the things you are talking about (especially information about physical exams and insurance). Allow time for the boys to ask questions. Be sure to get the name, address and phone number of each boy who expresses a desire to play. Meetings of this type should go far in getting your future players properly introduced to your style of football.

Check with Doctors Concerning Physical Exams During the Summer

If you have one or more team doctors, contact them now and suggest dates this summer for football physicals. Realize that a doctor's schedule is very busy and the earlier a date is set for physical exams the better chance you have of getting near the date you want. Make your doctors aware that it is necessary to inform your players soon of the summer physical date before school is out and they get separated for the summer.

Also, ask the doctors for suggestions for making the summer physicals run smoother. For example, where would they prefer having the exams? In a classroom? In the football locker room? Are scales for weighing and measuring height needed? What about nurses to assist the doctors? It would be a good idea to record important decisions as shown in Figure 4-5. Refer to this information throughout the summer and send a reminder copy of the information to all doctors concerned several weeks before the exams.

Plan Football Program, Including Selling Ads and Selecting a Printer

In some schools the handling of football programs, selling advertisements for the programs, and selecting a printer is handled by the TD (Booster) Club. But if the job falls to the coach now is the time to get started. Here are some suggestions:

PHYSICAL EXAM:
School _____ Date of Exam _____19____
Head Coach _____ Time of Exam _____a.m./p.m.
Location of Exam: Building _____Room number _____
Names of Doctors to attend: _____
_____
_____
_____

Doctor in charge _____His phone No. _____
Items needed (scales, tables, etc.): _____
_____
_____

Approximate number of players receiving physical exams: _____
Names of nurses who will assist: _____
_____
_____

Figure 4-5

1. Contact several printing firms and inquire about prices for printing the number of programs you will need. Be sure to specify how many pages will be in the program as this is where the cost adds up. Show each printer a copy of last fall's program to give him an idea of what you want.

2. Once the cost has been determined begin selling ads for the program. There should be a variety of ad sizes and prices. For example, a full-page ad might cost $100, a half-page ad $50, a quarter-page ad for $25, etc. Inside cover, back page, or other places where ads will be especially noticeable may cost more.

3. Start by getting reorders on the same ads that were in the program last fall. Clip each individual ad and either take it personally to the owner of the business, or mail it to him. Ask if there are any changes in the ad such as new phone numbers. Also find out if he wishes to enlarge his ad.

4. Some teams use cheerleaders or players themselves to handle several ads apiece, and to see that the money is collected.

5. After a majority of the ads are sold take the ads to the printer so that he can start his layout. Remind him of the approximate number of player and cheerleader photos that will be added after they are taken in the late summer.

6. Send a letter to the coach of each team that plays at your school this fall. Remind him to send a player roster as soon as possible after his players reassemble for fall practice.

(Realistically, don't expect these program rosters until fall practice starts. The printer can add them last, just before the programs are printed.)

7. The selling of ads, and working with the printer to produce a good program, will take some time. By beginning now, much of the work can be finished before fall practice begins.

Make List of Stadium Repairs
to Be Done During the Summer

Prepare a list of stadium repairs that will be needed before the start of the fall season and give the list to the school maintenance people. This will allow three to four months for the materials to be bought and the work to be done, yet will present a new and fresh look to your stadium for the first game. Talk first with the school principal or perhaps the Board of Education about funds available for stadium repairs. Also get their ideas of repairs to be done. Keep a chart like the one in Figure 5-1. It will help follow the progress of your stadium repair project. (See page 66.)

Save the lists from year to year. You may want to look back and determine when certain repairs were made.

Plan Repairs and Servicing of School Vehicles
During the Summer

Most schools usually have one or several types of vehicles for exclusive use of the football team. It may be a 45-60 passenger bus, a van, a truck, a car or a combination of several of these. Make plans now to service each vehicle during the summer months when there is less demand for use of the vehicle. Start by taking a careful

Repairs	Date started	Date completed	Comments
Front gate			
Press box roof			
Door to visitor's dressing room			
Hot water heater in Home dressing room			
Replace broken seats			
Repaint goal post			
Replace scoreboard lights			

Figure 5-1

look at each form of transportation. Does it need tires? Brake repairs? New muffler? New battery? New belts and hoses? Do all outside lights work well? When was the last engine tune-up?

Contact a reliable auto (truck, bus) repair shop. Make an appointment to bring the vehicle in during a certain period of the summer. (Note: check with all coaches beforehand to be sure that no one has plans to use the vehicle.) Give as much information as possible to the repair shop people concerning what type work is to be done so that they can use the next few weeks to locate the proper tires, battery, etc. needed for the vehicle. Be sure to keep accurate records each year listing everything done to each vehicle. File these in the school office so that other coaches won't duplicate your repairs when they are not needed.

Reorder Stationery

If you ordered a year's supply of athletic stationery it should be about exhausted by now. Since the printing of good stationery might take several weeks before it is delivered go ahead and place your order for next fall. Here are a few things to think about:

1. Well-designed and printed stationery is a good reflection on your school (and football team).

2. The lettering should be in school colors, not just black and white.
3. Include your team mascot or emblem on the letterhead and/or envelope.
4. Some like to list the names of all coaches on the letterhead. This is all right . . . until one assistant leaves the staff.
5. List your coaches' office phone numbers on the letterhead.
6. You may want to list other pieces of information on the letterhead, such as *State Champions*, or *Member—Region 2-AAAA*.

Repair and Add to Weight Room Equipment

Since many coaches will have their athletes working during the summer months to prepare for the season, now seems to be the best time to make additions and repairs. The weight equipment will certainly be in use during the school months, so here, at the end of the year, is an excellent time to slow down, or stop if necessary, all weight room work in order to improve the equipment.

First, make a careful check of each piece of equipment. Note where improvements are needed. If the school athletic year has been a good one financially, there might even be money available for new equipment. Engage the help of all players to clean each piece of equipment. Add lubricants where needed. These improvements should have the weight room in excellent shape to start summer or fall workouts.

Two-week Indoctrination Course
In Football Leadership

Here in May, just before school is out and players separate for the summer, is a good time to have a two-week indoctrination in football leadership. Not all team members should be chosen for these unique meetings. The number which you and your staff wish to invite to the leadership meetings will depend on many things— overall size of the squad, number of potential leaders available, past performances of returning players—just to name a few. Suggestions for selecting players:

1. Select those who are *already* leaders. You may have none, one or ten.

2. Select players who have been loyal to the football program for one or more years.
3. Select some younger, as well as older, players.
4. Select some of the team's better athletes.
5. Select some team members who are intelligent, mature, and who do well in their school work.

Set a time convenient for those selected (as well as for the coaches), perhaps in the evening. Sit down informally with the potential leaders. Hear their views concerning their team. Talk with them about why *good* leadership is necessary. Discuss ways of being good leaders, both on and off the field (in the locker room). Discuss frankly with them the goals for the coming season and ask for suggestions for reaching these goals. Let each player (leader) set personal goals relating to how he can best contribute leadership to the team. Remind them that one player might lead by example on the field (hustling, all out effort), while another leads by talking quietly with a teammate before a game.

Give the players in the leadership group some experience in leading others. For example, give one player each day the responsibility of starting the meeting, keeping order if others talk too loud or out of turn, and perhaps leading the group through light exercise. The coaching staff should offer suggestions to improve his leadership.

At the end of the two-week session challenge the leaders to lead the way in encouraging summer workouts, to call those who are absent, to discourage comments that are detrimental to the football program, and to not tolerate among themselves players who won't work.

Hopefully, at the end of the two weeks the coaching staff will know whom they can depend on as the true team leaders for the up-coming season.

Final Check to Be Sure Game Contracts and Officials Contract Have Been Signed and Returned

This item of business was on the agenda for February and should have been completed then. However, a final check is a good idea because after this month coaches, principals, and other school officials, as well as game officials, are gone for the summer. Trying to reach them may be difficult. It would be a disaster next fall to find a confusion of dates with an opponent or to find no officials at your home opener. Signed contracts, properly filed after checking all dates and arrangements, can eliminate this worry.

Meet with Newly Elected Cheerleaders and Sponsor

In many schools cheerleaders are elected in the spring for the following school year. Whether you realize it or not they seek and need your approval since they will be working with and for your team. Take the first opportunity to congratulate each girl personally, either with a letter or in person. Let each one know that you know her by name and recognize her on campus.

Set up a meeting with all the girls and their sponsor. Tell them of your plans for the summer, such as when you plan to be around school (in case they need supplies, rosters, etc.). Go over the football schedule and discuss plans for out-of-town games (travel, meals, etc). Talk about home games, especially Homecoming.

Then give them a chance to ask you questions. They'll want to know your ideas on pep rallies and many other things. Consider letting the cheerleaders bring a small bulletin board and place it near the locker room. Encourage them to keep the bulletin board filled with notes of encouragement to the players, photos, plans for pep rallies, etc. This is an excellent way to make the cheerleaders feel part of the team. They can do a lot for your team if you'll just show them a little interest.

Check Chains and Down Marker for Repairs

Get this small task out of the way now so it won't be on your mind in the fall. Start by looking at the set of chains. Paint them if necessary. Be sure the chains are attached tightly to the poles. *Measure* the distance between poles to be sure of an accurate ten-yard measurement. If one or several lengths of chain are missing the distance will not be accurate and a minor repair now could save arguments later.

Check the paint job on the down marker. There is no reason to have a chipped or flaked down marker when there is time now to paint it so that it is clearly visible.

Check with Camera Man Concerning
Next Fall's Game Films

Contact your film man. Get a commitment from him to handle your game films next fall. (This commitment may need to be in writing, especially if a payment of money is involved.) Decide exactly what the camera man is responsible for doing. Will he pick up the film or will you? Who brings the camera to the games? How will he travel to out-of-town games? Will he eat pre-game and/or post-game meals with the team? Will he get paid? If so, how much? When will the payments be made (after each game or at the season's end)? Who carries the film to be developed after the game? Who picks it up and when? If the film turns out poorly will the camera man be paid the full amount? Answers to these and other quetsions should be decided now, not after the season starts and you have a thousand other things on your mind.

If time permits, show a few of the films from last season. Point out things you liked and didn't like. Was the picture too dark or too light? Do you prefer more close-up shots or do you like to see the entire offense and defense in the picture? Most coaches don't like shots of the band or the crowd in the game films. While these people are appreciated, the fact remains that film is expensive and must be directed on the game at all times. This also insures that the film isn't used up before the game ends.

If camera repairs are needed, decide who is to be in charge of taking the camera to the repair shop and picking it up. Also discuss how payment for repairs will be handled.

Make List of Summer Addresses
and Phone Numbers of Players

Although you may have made previous lists of players and phone numbers, now is the time to do it again. Many players will not be at home during the summer. They will visit grandparents, aunts and uncles, sometimes for several weeks or maybe two months. Others will be at various camps. A family vacation may last a weekend or several weeks.

Call a meeting of all team members. Have them complete a list giving the information shown in Figure 5-2. Make extra copies of this list. Give them to all coaches and perhaps even to the school principal or guidance counselor. (School officials may need to locate a player about grades or eligibility requirements.) Hand out copies of the addresses and phone numbers to all players, or at least to the team leaders. This will encourage players to keep in contact with their teammates.

Name of Player _____Permanent Phone No. _____
Permanent Address _____
  (A) Summer Phone No. _____
      Summer Address _____
      Dates at this Location _____
      Reason for being at this address _____
  (B) Summer Phone No. _____
      Summer Address _____
      Dates at this Location _____
      Reason for being at this address _____

Figure 5-2

On the line which says *Reason for being at this address* the player should put "visiting relatives" or "attending summer camp." If no phone numbers of addresses are available this summer (perhaps player will be traveling daily) the player should list the phone numbers of relatives who might have occasion to be in touch with him.

Check Out Special Equipment (Footballs, Kicking Tees) for Players to Use During the Summer

Encourage your players to work on their own during the summer months especially quarterbacks, centers, snappers, receivers, and kickers. Provide them with the necessary balls and tees. If your practice field or stadium is usually locked, set up a time (such as every Monday, Wednesday, and Friday from 4:00 pm to 6:00 pm) to have it open. Assign assistant coaches to help you keep the fields open, especially when you are out of town. Be sure to keep an accurate chart (see Figure 5-3, on page 72) of who has checked out school football equipment.

Under *Other Issued*, list items such as kicking shoes. Under *Coach*, have the coach who issued the equipment place his initials.

Player	Football Issued	Kicking tee Issued	Other Issued	Date Issued	Date Returned	Coach

Figure 5-3

Make Sure All Ordered Equipment Has Been Delivered or Can Be Received During the Summer Months

Before leaving for the summer vacation carefully review all orders for equipment. Certainly you will find some orders that have not been delivered. Many of these orders involve items that will be needed in August, when fall practice starts. Use a chart like the one in Figure 5-4 to keep up with all items that you are expecting in during the summer.

Equipment ordered: _____

Date ordered: _____ 19____

Company: _____

Address: _____City: _____ State: _____

Approximate date expected for equipment to arrive: _____

(Below: Use only if equipment is to be received by someone other than the football coach.)

Upon arrival call: _____Phone No. _____

Store equipment in _____until picked up by the coach.

Figure 5-4

If the equipment will be sent directly to the coach at his office (or at his home), fill out the top five lines (from *Equipment Ordered* to *Approximate date* . . .). Keep the information handy so that it will serve as a reminder to watch for, and expect, the shipment during the summer.

If the equipment might be delivered with other mail and packages to the general school office, fill out duplicate charts and leave with the principal, school secretary, custodian, etc. *Be sure to fill out the bottom of the chart.* When the equipment is delivered, school personnel will know whom to call and where to keep it stored until picked up.

Order Small Printed Schedules of Football Games
to Hand Out to Students in the Fall

Contact a local businessman and offer him the opportunity to supply billfold-size schedule cards with his own advertisement on the card. The cards are usually very inexpensive and can be ordered by the hundreds. Many merchants would like to have their company name on the often-looked-at cards. Take the schedule and the ad to a print shop. Tell them the date you want the cards ready (usually late July or early August). In the fall, when school starts, be sure every student gets one (or several) of the cards.

If space permits, list local college or professional schedules on the card. Or, if you prefer, list the high school basketball schedule on the back side. Be sure to plan to pick the cards up during the summer, and, of course, send a thank you note to the sponsor of the cards.

Arrange to Have Fields Watered During the Summer

Check with school maintenance people to be sure that all equipment needed to water the field during the summer will be available. This might mean only water hose and sprinklers at some schools, but might involve heavy movable pipes at other places. Be sure to have proper tools if pipes need to be connected or disconnected and moved.

Check the summer schedules of assistant coaches to determine who will be available during the summer months of June and July to keep the fields watered. Perhaps a posted list in the coaches' office would help remind them of the schedule.

Arrange for Grass to Be Cut and Kept Free of Litter

Some schools have maintenance crews or custodial people who tend to this. If this is your situation, you need to keep them informed as to how often you wish the grass cut. This will depend on your summer workout schedule (if you plan to use the field).

If the grass cutting is left to the coaching staff, be sure you have access to all grass cutting equipment. Also get the phone numbers of people whom you can call on if repairs are needed on the mowers. As with the field watering schedule, check with assistant coaches and determine who can help with this chore and who is responsible for each week during the summer.

Talk with Each Team Member Concerning Team Goals and Individual Goals for the Coming Season

Before the players break away for the summer try to talk with each player concerning his personal goals for the fall. Encourage him, also, to think of team goals to work for. Here are some points to consider:

1. Set *realistic* goals. Do not encourage the 5'6", 120 lb., sophomore, 4th team QB to set as his goal to become a first team All-State QB this fall. Instead, encourage him to work toward becoming *his* team's first team QB.

2. Use *figures* to relate to the goals. A receiver might work toward catching 30 passes. An offensive lineman may work toward grading above 80% in at least 7 games. A quarterback might seek to complete at least 60% of his passes. A defensive back could try to intercept at least 6 passes.

3. Have the player *write down* his goals, giving a copy to the coach who works directly with him (such as backfield coach), to you as head coach, and keeping one for himself.

4. Remind the player of his goals during early fall workouts.

5. Remind him again just before the first game and again midway through the season.

As far as *team* goals are concerned, you might want the players to meet as a group and decide their season goals. Again, be realistic but be careful not to dampen their enthusiasm. For a team that was 1-9 last fall and has only a few returning lettermen to set their goal towards the state title might only be fooling themselves and cause them to lose faith in their goal as soon as an inevitable loss occurs early in the season. Encourage them to set their goal at a break-even (5-5) season, or maybe a winning (6-4) season. Tell the team this is not to say that you *expect* them to lose 4 or 5 games but that a break-even or winning season would be a step up for the program and that the following year a play-off slot or a title would be within range. If the players then insist on setting their goals higher than you feel are realistic, just turn them loose; maybe they will make it!

Clean and Disinfect Locker Room

Just before school is out for the summer have the custodians thoroughly clean and disinfect the locker room. It is a good idea to remove as much equipment, tables, etc. as possible before they start. Be sure to also clean closets, shower areas, and equipment rooms. Special care should be given to the training room, especially equipment such as the whirlpool.

While you have the custodians working with you, go ahead and set up a schedule for regular cleaning and disinfecting during the coming school year. You will need their services more during the fall football season (and during spring practice, if you have it) than at other times during the year.

End-of-School Football Players Meeting as a Team

This meeting is of great importance and should be well advertised so that every team member will be present. The general purpose of the meeting is to touch base with team members before the summer break so that every player will know precisely what is expected of him during the summer, and to conclude any unfinished business relating to the present year. Here is a checklist of some things that might be covered:

1. Be sure any player who has not filled out an *Equipment Size Card* (See Chapter 4—April) gets one, fills it out, and returns it before leaving. This will help in sizing player's helmets, jerseys, etc. during the summer months.

2. Be sure all *summer addresses* and *phone numbers* are still correct (these were compiled earlier in this chapter).

3. Collect *individual* and *team goals* from those who have not turned them in.

4. Stress working hard on *final grades* which will determine eligibility for the fall.

5. Announce the date for late summer *physical exams* (if given by local doctors to the team as a group). Remind the players that failure to get this "team physical" means they must get their own physical at their own expense.

6. Review the fall *insurance* plan. Remind players of the cost of the insurance so that they can have the money available when practice starts in late summer.

7. Review *summer workout* and/or weight room schedule.

8. Stress the *starting date* for fall practice.

9. Remind each player individually which *level of team* he is to begin practice with in the fall. Some will be on the varsity while others will play junior varsity. This is especially important to marginal players who might be unsure where they stand.

10. Hand out season *schedules* for the fall.

11. Give preliminary information concerning fall football *camp* (see Chapter 8—August).

12. *Weight* and *height* measurements of each player should be taken. (Take these again in the first days of fall practice and compare the growth of each player.)

13. Be sure to find out if any players plan *vacations* that would make them late for the first days of fall practice.

14. Provide each player with *phone numbers, addresses*, and places of summer *employment* (if any) *of each coach* so that a player can make quick contact with any coach at any time during the summer.

Reminder: Jot down the names of any players who are absent so that contact can be made with them individually concerning the items covered in the team meeting.

Carefully Check Final Grades of Players for Eligibility Requirements

As soon as final exams have been taken coaches should begin checking final grades for all players to determine their scholastic eligibility for the coming fall season. Here is a sample plan to follow:

1. Several weeks before school is out ask each player to fill out a card showing his schedule, class period, room number, and teacher. This information might be obtained easily from the office in some schools, rather than having the players do it.

2. Either (a) visit each teacher in school personally, or (b) have assistant coaches visit different school departments (math, English, social studies, P.E., etc).

3. Ask the teacher to help by providing the final grade for those football players he or she teaches. In many schools the coach will not need the exact grade, just whether or not the player *passed* or *failed*.

4. Explain to the teacher your reason for wanting to know the grade as soon as possible. (The reason is that any player who fails a course needs to register for summer school in order to make up the course and be eligible for the fall football season. Some players have been known to "get away" for the summer thinking they "passed everything." They then return home in mid-summer only to find that they are not eligible scholastically and that summer school is half over.)

5. Be sure to thank the teacher for taking time to help!

6. Contact immediately any player who is in trouble scholastically and review eligibility requirements with him and his parents.

Compile and Prepare Records and Statistics for This Fall's Football Program

If your present football program doesn't contain a page showing *past* records and statistics for your school, you are missing a very interesting item that can greatly increase program sales. Try these suggestions:

1. Begin searching for team records and individual statistics. Begin with last fall's stats and work *backward* through the years, going as far back in your team's history as possible.

2. Sources of information for these records and stats can be newspapers, radio or TV stations, school annuals, former players, state record books, and older fans.

3. Stop when you reach a point in time where *accurate* records can no longer be found.

4. Here are examples of records and stats to use:

- *Yearly won-loss records.* Example: 1981 . . . 9-1, 1980 . . . 8-2, 1979 . . .5-5
- *Championships and titles won.* Example: State Champions . . . 1976, 1971, 1962; City Champions . . . 1981, 1978, 1976, 1972
- *Most consecutive wins.* Example: 24, from 1970-72
- *Best season record.* Example: 13-0 in 1976

- *Most shutouts by defensive team* (one season). Example: 8
- *Most points scored (one game).* Example: 62, against _____ High School in 1970
- *Most points scored in one season.* Example: 345 in 1981
- *Longest run from scrimmage.* Example: Stewart McElwaney 1971 . . . 97 yds. vs. _____ High School
- *Most single season yards rushing.* Example: Andy Ullrich . . . 1971 . . . 1623 yds.
- *Most career yards rushing.* Example: Randy Byers . . . 1966, 1967, 1968 . . . 3002 yds.
  (Note: add passing and defensive records and stats along with kicking information.)

5. Be careful not to use any records or stats that can not be verified. This would only lead to arguments and tend to challenge the accuracy of the other records.

6. Add a statement such as this one at the top of your record and stat page: *These records and statistics, dating back to 1956, are accurate to the best of our knowledge. We encourage anyone to help bring these stats up to date by supplying documented evidence of earlier records.* A note of this type will help the feelings of some "old timer" who might wonder why his 1947 rushing record isn't included. (If he can show proof that his record was better, add it next season!)

7. Since this page will be widely read by fans who buy football programs, an advertisement listed on this page should bring top dollar.

Make Sure Those Players Needing Summer School for Eligibility Have Signed Up Properly

After all final grades are recorded make sure that all players needing to attend summer school to be eligible have registered properly. Double-check their summer schedules to be sure the course(s) they are taking will carry enough hours to complete eligibility requirements.

Once the player has entered summer school the coach needs to run the same checks on his grades as he normally would do during the school year. If possible, confer with the summer school teacher on each player's progress. Keep up with the attendance of each player as many summer schools drop students from their rolls after a minimum number of absences.

Call Photographer to Set Up an Appointment for Team
and Individual Photos to Be Made in August

Most photographers schedule photo sessions weeks ahead. Weddings, parties, and other special events can crowd a schedule especially just before practice starts in August. Now is the time to contact the photographer and set up a picture day schedule. Give him complete details of what you want. This will enable him to come better equipped with color cameras, black and white film, extra help, etc. Give him a list such as the one in Figure 6-1.

Date: _____ School: _____
Address: _____Phone:_____
Person in charge of team: Coach _____
Pictures needed:
  (a)   Team picture . . . Color . . . 35 copies
  (b)   Cheerleaders . . . Color . . . 10 copies
  (c)   Coaching Staff . . . Color . . . 6 copies
  (d)   Individual players . . . black and white . . . one each
  (e)   Managers . . . black and white . . . one each
  (f)   Individual Senior players . . . Color . . . one each
  (g)   Captains and Coaches . . . Color . . . 8 copies
Remake date will be: _____
Date photos are needed: _____

Figure 6-1

By setting up picture day two months in advance, the coach will be able to better plan his early fall practice sessions so that picture day (in August) will cause as little confusion as possible.

Contact Members of the Press and Tell Them
When Picture Day Will Be Held

Once a picture day date has been confirmed with the photographer, call local newspapers and give them the date. We feel this is very important for two reasons. First, it lets the press know that you are thinking of them and including them in your football plans. Second, issuing game pants, jerseys, etc. is time-consuming and often takes away from practice time. If the press is present at picture day, they can get all the pictures they need for the newspaper coverage, and will not be asking you to "suit up" the players several weeks later when you don't have the time. If any other organizations will be needing pictures during the season, be sure to inform them to be present. This group might include the school newspaper and/or yearbook. Be sure to remind them that if photos are not taken now they will be extremely difficult to get later (once the season starts).

Plan Budget for the Coming School Year

The football coach is often the Athletic Director and has the responsibility of planning an athletic budget for the school year. Even if the football coach is not the AD, football is usually the biggest source of revenue in the athletic department. In order to run a sound football program, the coach must have a good knowledge of the school athletic budget. He should know how much money is taken in from every sporting event. He must be aware of the needs of not only his own program, but of the basketball team, baseball team, cheerleaders, etc.

June is an excellent month to set up a budget for the coming school year. School is out and the coach has more time to spend with budget matters.

There are a great number of things that can effect a proposed budget. If gate receipts are greater than expected, or a football playoff game (extra revenue) develops, there will be more money to spend and will allow for a "loosening up" of the budget. If bad weather cuts into football receipts, the budget might need to be tightened.

By using the budget plan shown in Figure 6-2, the athletic department should be able to keep finances in their proper prospective throughout the entire year. (See page 82.)

Note: Be sure to ask the help of all coaches of all sports as you develop the budget.

Be sure to alter the budget (shown in Figure 6-2) slightly to fit the needs of your particular school.

After the football season is over review the budget. If you made 20% more in football than anticipated, you might wish to raise each sport's allowed expenses by 20%. Or you might want to save the money for next year. Keep in mind that basketball income might be lower than anticipated so it might be wise to save the money. If football income was *down* 10% from the estimated income, you might warn all head coaches of all sports that their budget will be cut by 10%.

PROPOSED BUDGET

School ——————————————————————————Year ——————————

INCOME:

Football Gate Receipts (Anticipated)
    Season Tickets $———————
    1st Home Game $———————
    2nd Home Game $———————
    3rd Home Game $———————
    4th Home Game $———————
    5th Home Game $———————
    Guarantees $———————
      Total Football Gate Receipts (Anticipated) $———————

Miscellaneous Receipts (Anticipated)
    Football Program Sales $———————
    Booster Club $———————
      Total Miscellaneous Receipts (Anticipated) $———————

Basketball Gate Receipts (Anticipated)
    Ten Home Games $———————
    Tournament $———————
      Total Basketball Gate Receipts (Anticipated) $———————
Wrestling Gate Receipts (Anticipated)
    Five Home Matches $———————
      Total Wrestling Gate Receipts (Anticipated) $———————

Baseball Gate Receipts (Anticipated)
    Seven Home Games $———————
      Total Baseball Gate Receipts (Anticipated) $———————

TOTAL FOOTBALL, MISCELLANEOUS, BASKETBALL, WRESTLING,
AND BASEBALL GATE RECEIPTS (Anticipated) $———————

EXPENSES:

Note—Estimates of expenses are based on present prices.

General Expenses
    Dues $———————
    Telephone $———————
    Stationery $———————
    Stamps and Postage $———————
    Other $———————
      Total General Expenses $———————

Football
Insurance $_____
Tickets $_____
Filming $_____
Officials $_____
Travel $_____
Meals $_____
Scouting $_____
Medical Supplies $_____
Equipment $_____
Awards and Letters $_____
   Total Football Expenses $_____

Basketball
Transportation $_____
Meals $_____
Scouting $_____
Medical Supplies $_____
Equipment $_____
Awards and Letters $_____
   Total Basketball Expenses $_____

Wrestling
Transportation $_____
Meals $_____
Mat Repairs $_____
Equipment $_____
Awards and Letters $_____
   Total Wrestling Expenses $_____

Baseball
Transportation $_____
Equipment $_____
Umpires $_____
Awards and Letters $_____
   Total Baseball Expenses $_____

Track
Transportation $_____
Equipment $_____
Awards and Letters $_____
   Total Track Expenses $_____

Golf
Green Fees $_____
Golf Balls $_____
   Total Golf Expenses $_____

TOTAL EXPENSES FOR ALL SPORTS $_____
TOTAL FOOTBALL, MISCELLANEOUS, BASKET-
BALL, WRESTLING, AND BASEBALL GATE
RECEIPTS (Anticipated) $_____
ANTICIPATED YEAR END BALANCE $_____

Figure 6-2

Arrange Vehicles for Transportation to
Football Camp in August

If you plan to take your team to a week of pre-season football practice away from home (see *Football Camp Checklist*, Chapter 8—August), now is the time to arrange your travel plans. You will probably need some combination (but perhaps not all) of the following:

1. Bus—The team should travel together in the minimum number of vehicles possible. This means one or two large buses depending on team size. You might also use one bus to carry football equipment, bags and suitcases, dummies, and medical equipment. If your team doesn't have athletic-department-owned buses, you probably can arrange with city or county school officials to provide school buses.

2. Van—A nine-to-twelve passenger van can be used for coaches, small medicine kits, bags of footballs, etc. It also provides for short trips at camp, such as going into town.

3. Car—It never hurts to have a car at camp. It could be used to take a player to the doctor, or to provide transportation back home in case of emergency involving a player or coach.

4. Truck—Could be used to transport equipment, suitcases, dummies, or even your two-man sled. Be sure a covering is available if the truck is not enclosed.

School officials, Booster Club members, fans, and parents, are sources that the coach can call on to help locate the needed transportation. If cars, vans, or trucks are borrowed from individuals be sure to check on insurance.

Begin Summer Work with Quarterback,
Receivers, Kickers, etc.

Now that school is out, the coaches should be able to get together with specialist groups to improve on their individual skills and not have to be too concerned with school schedules, meetings, etc. This will allow plenty of time for one-on-one instruction between coach and player.

Each coach needs to work out a schedule with his players that best suits their time schedule. Some may prefer to work out early in the morning, around 7:00 a.m. when it is cool. Others may prefer late in the evening. Have a set routine, or practice schedule, to follow. Know what you want to accomplish. If possible, conduct the workouts in the game stadium. Every chance these specialists get to work in "game surroundings" will be beneficial.

Make Final Review of Offense and Defense to Be Used in the Fall

Although a number of meetings have undoubtedly been held in the winter and spring months (and during spring practice, if held,) concerning offensive and defensive plans for the fall, a final check of these plans should be made. Perhaps some players you were counting on in key positions have moved. Some players may have failed schoolwork and will be ineligible. Others may not have recovered from injuries as rapidly as you had hoped and may not be able to play.

By reviewing these offensive and defensive plans now, you still have about two months to make alterations. There is still plenty of time to study, watch more film, install new techniques, or do anything else necessary to change your plans for the fall season. *Note:* Be careful not to make too many drastic changes that will leave the players confused and disorganized on the first day of practice.

Inform all coaches of any changes in personnel or technique. Do not wait until the opening day of practice to announce new plans. Also, inform key people like quarterbacks, or defensive captains, of changes.

Paint and/or Repair 7-Man Sled, 2-Man Sled, Lineman Chutes and Goalposts

If you want your players to perform in a first-class manner, your facilities should look first class. Of course, it isn't possible to always obtain new equipment. But you can make your available equipment *look* like new.

There are certainly a number of coaches whose summer schedules will provide time to make repairs on the practice field equipment. A good paint job on practice field sleds, chutes, and goalposts, will give your program a first-class look. Paint these items in your school colors. (Some schools like to paint items such as blocking sleds in the school colors of their major opponent.)

Clean Out Office Desk and
Bring Files Up to Date

This is a good time to re-evaluate all printed material located in the football office. If space permits, begin by taking every piece of literature out of the room. Remove everything from the files, but be careful to keep it in order. Once the room is emptied of all written material clean the room thoroughly. Then review each piece of paper, each notebook, and each memo carefully. Replace valuable and usable material neatly in its place in the coaches' office. Throw away old, outdated material. Keep several boxes nearby and place material which is not needed at the moment in the boxes (this material would include old statistics, old letters, receipts, etc). Stack the boxes of old material in a storeroom near the office (be sure to label the boxes indicating what each contains).

This is also a good time to bring your filing system up to date. Arrange it so that material can be instantly located. Keep in mind that all material in the coaches' office should be arranged so that staff members can locate items they need (such as scouting forms) quickly.

Mimeograph Statistic Sheets That Will Be
Used in the Fall

There are many ways to keep statistics and each coach usually has his own system. We have found the stat sheet (Figure 6-3, starting on page 87) simple to keep and very informative. Whatever system you use to suit your needs is fine. But now is the time to type out your forms and mimeograph enough for the season.

Prepare Charts Showing Offensive and
Defensive Goals for the Season

Make two large charts and place them in the center of the locker room bulletin board or in some other area that is seen *every* day by *all* players. These charts list the defensive and offensive goals for each game of the season (see Figure 6-4 on page 89).

STATISTIC SHEET

_____ HIGH vs. _____ HIGH Date: _____ 19____

AT _____ Score _____

RUSHING:

Player	Rushing Yardage	Total Carries	Total Yds.

(_Explanation:_ Under "player" write each ball carrier's number, such as #37. If # 37 gains 6 yards, place, a +6 under Rushing Yardage. If he loses 2 put −2 under Rushing Yardage. At the end of the game list his Total Carries and Yards.)

PASSING:

Passer	Attempts	Completed	Yards	Totals

(_Explanation:_ Under "passer" place the number of the passer. Make a mark under each "attempt" and "completed." Write in the Yards such as +18, +23, etc. Totals at the end of the line should read something like 14/8/144 indicating attempts, completed, and yardage.

RECEIVING:

Receiver	No. of Catches	Yards	TDs	Totals

PUNTING:

Punter	No. of Kicks	Yards	Average

SPECIAL PLAYS:

Player	Special play (interception, fumble recovery, blocked kick)

(_Explanation:_ If a player makes a special play, list first his jersey number under "player." Then put down something like _Interception /1/ 22 yds._ This indicates the player intercepted one pass and returned it 22 yds. Indicate the same for a fumble recovery or blocked kick.)

FIRST DOWNS:
_____ High: _____Total 1st Downs: _____
_____ High: _____Total 1st Downs: _____
(*Explanation:* Put name of your high school on the first line followed by a
mark for each first down. Do the same for your opponent on the second line.)

OPPONENT'S RUSHING:
_____
_____
_____
_____
(*Explanation:* Simply mark +3, +4, −1, +3, etc. to indicate the rushing
yardage of your opponent.)

OPPONENT'S PASSING:

Attempted	Completed	Yards	Totals

(*Explanation:* Make a mark under "attempted" each time a pass is thrown,
and under "completed" if caught. Under "yardage" put +13, +9, etc. Totals
should read something like 15/6/133, indicating attempts/completions/
yards.)

FINAL TOTAL YARDAGE:

School	Rushing	Passing	Total Yardage

SCORING:

Player	Touchdown	Extra Point	Field Goal	Other	Total Pts.

(*Explanation:* When a player scores put his jersey number under "player." If
he has scored a TD, put down something like *6 Yard Run* or *22 Yard Pass
from #10*. Mark his other appropriate columns if needed.)

SCORE BY QUARTERS:

School	1st QT.	2nd QT.	3rd QT.	4th QT.	Final Score

DEFENSE:

Player	Tackles	Assists	Total Tackles	Total Assists

PUNT RETURNS:
Player	No. of Returns	Yards	Average

KICKOFF RETURNS:
Player	No. of Returns	Yards	Average

Figure 6-3

First, sit down with your coaching staff (and maybe some of your team leaders) and determine what you feel it will take to defeat the teams on your schedule. Make your goals tough, but realistic. Beside each goal provide a slot for each game on your schedule where you can write *Yes* indicating *Yes, we reached this goal*, or *No*, indicating *No, we did not reach this goal*. These two charts will constantly remind players of what it takes to win, and will allow them to keep up with their game-to-game performances. Figure 6-4 illustrates the type of defensive and offensive goals that we use on our charts.

DEFENSIVE OBJECTIVES

19____   _____ High School

Goal	1st Game	2nd Game	3rd Game	4th Game	5th Game	6th Game	7th Game	(etc)
Held Opponent scoreless:								
Held Opp. under 150 yards rushing:								
Held Opp. under 75 yards passing:								
No run over 20 yards:								
No pass over 30 yards:								
Recover two fumbles:								
Intercept two passes:								
Two QB sacks:								
No punt return over 15 yards:								
No more than 20 yards in defensive penalties:								
Block one punt, EP, or FG:								
Stop Opp. inside our 10 yard line at least 1 time:								

Goal	1st Game	2nd Game	3rd Game	4th Game	5th Game	6th Game	7th Game	(etc)
Make Opp. punt inside their 20 yard line at least once:								
No touchdown passes:								
Hold Opp. to less than 7 first downs:								

OFFENSIVE OBJECTIVES

19____   _____ High School

Goal	1st Game	2nd Game	3rd Game	4th Game	5th Game	6th Game	7th Game	(etc)
Rush for over 200 yds:								
Pass for over 100 yds:								
Complete over 6 passes:								
No fumbles lost:								
No pass interceptions:								
No punt, EP, FG, blocked:								
Two runs over 25 yds:								
Two passes over 30 yds.								
Score 21 or more pts.								
No QB sacks:								
At least 1 TD pass:								
One punt return over 25 yards:								
No more than 20 yds. in offensive penalties:								
Score each time inside Opp. 10 yard line:								
At least 10 first downs:								

Figure 6-4

Mimeograph Scouting Forms

Take time now to prepare the scouting forms that you will need for the up-coming season. The form shown in Figure 6-5 is the form which we feel gives a good *general* picture of the team you are scouting. If you are able to easily get *films* of your opponents, this form will be all you need. Plays, blocking assignments, pass routes, etc. can be taken from the film. However, *if films of your opponent are not available*, use the form shown in Figure 6-5 *plus* diagram as many of the plays as possible of your opponent. The form which starts below is designed to give a *broad picture* of your opponent, and in some cases provides information which can't be gathered from the film (such as rating team enthusiasm).

SCOUTING REPORT

Team Scouted: _____ Score: _____ Date: _____
Their Opponent: _____ Score: _____ Location: _____
Name of Scout: _____
Stats: (taken from newspaper the next morning)

	1st Downs	Yards Rushing	Yards Passing	Passes Attempted	Passes Comp.	Punt Ave.
Team Scouted:						
Their Opp.:						

GENERAL INFORMATION:
Are they a good team in overall ability?

(Circle one)	1	2	3	4	5
	(great)	(good)	(ave)	(fair)	(poor)

Rate their team speed: 1 2 3 4 5
Rate their team size: 1 2 3 4 5
General team organization and discipline: 1 2 3 4 5
Name, number, size of their two best backs:
_____
_____

Name, number and size of their two best linemen:
_____
_____

Is their offense built on Passing?____ Power?____ Speed?____
Any injuries to their players which might hinder their play? _____
_____

Tell briefly what we must do in order to win the game:
_____
_____

Do they have a really outstanding player, one who can beat us unless we control him? If so, describe: _____
_____
_____

Do they show any unusual plays (such as reverses or halfback passes)? If so, diagram:

Diagram their favorite offensive set: List starters by position. Give name, jersey number, height, weight, and class in school.

Diagram their favorite defensive set. List starters at each position. Give name, jersey number, height, weight, and class in school:

Their offensive snap count: _____
Do they pull or trap with their guards very much? _____
Names and numbers of their two best pass receivers: _____
_____
Do they use motion? _____ Is motion effective? That is, do they throw to the motion man or use him as a key blocker, or is he just a decoy? _____
Who usually goes in motion? _____
Do they flip-flop the offensive line? _____
Do they flip their ends (split/tight) only? _____
On defense, do they stunt often? _____ Diagram:

Does their defense shift after the offense gets to the line of scrimmage? ___

Rate their defensive line:	1	2	3	4	5
Rate their linebackers:	1	2	3	4	5
Rate their defensive backs:	1	2	3	4	5

Give name, number, size, and class of their best:
  Defensive lineman: _____
  Linebacker: _____
  Defensive back: _____
Can we throwback on their defensive backs? _____
Do defensive ends crash or play soft? _____
Do they adjust well to motion? _____
Do they adjust to different line splits? _____
Do they rush the passer well? _____
What type goal line defense do they use? _____

| Rate the goal line defense? | | 1 | 2 | 3 | 4 | 5 |

Their kick-off man is number_____. His name is _____

| Rate his kick-offs: | Height | 1 | 2 | 3 | 4 | 5 |
| | Distance | 1 | 2 | 3 | 4 | 5 |

KO usually goes to the _____ yard line.
KO receiving: Do they return up the middle? _____
  Up the sideline? _____
  Do they reverse on their KO returns? _____
  Do they use no pattern? _____
Have they shown a quick kick? _____ If so, diagram:

Punting: Name and number of punter: _____

Rate his punts:	Height	1	2	3	4	5
	Distance	1	2	3	4	5
Rate the snapper:		1	2	3	4	5

How far back does the punter stand? _____yards
Punt receiving: Do they like to rush the punter? _____
Hold up our linemen? _____ Set up a return? _____
Who returns their punts? _____
Rate their punt return team: 1   2   3   4   5
SUMMARY: What team on our schedule are they comparable to?
_____

Were they enthusiastic and hustling? _____
Approximately how many players were dressed out? 20-30?_____ 30-40?
_____ 40-50? _____ Over 50?_____
Did they two-platoon on offense and defense? _____
What factors might have played a big part in the outcome of the game (such as bad weather, costly fumbles and interceptions, TD plays called back due to penalties, etc.)

Figure 6-5

Remember: If *no film* is available be sure that the scout diagrams as many offensive plays and defensive sets as possible. The form shown in Figure 6-5 can, for the most part, be filled out *after* the game.

Provide Cheerleader Bulletin Board in Dressing Room

Offer the cheerleaders the opportunity to put a bulletin board in or near the football dressing room. If your locker room has a hall leading to it this is a good place for the board. Players will see it as they approach the locker room. Cheerleaders will be able to put articles on it without going into the locker room. (*Note:* if the bulletin board must be in the locker room work out a time with the cheerleader sponsor for the cheerleaders to have access to the locker room before players come for practice.)

The bulletin board provides an opportunity for direct communication between players and cheerleaders. Encourage the cheerleaders to change the board every few days. The board can contain pictures, messages, announcements, plans for pep rallies, etc. Get the board up now so that the cheerleaders will have several weeks to plan ideas for the first week of practice.

Prepare Insurance List

In some schools the players must bring all or part of their insurance coverage premium. If possible, begin collecting this money and developing the insurance list so that it will be complete by the time you start fall practice. If the players do not have to pay any premium—perhaps the school handles the entire amount—go ahead and prepare the insurance list. Use the names of all players who (a) completed spring practice (if held), (b) have been working in the off-season conditioning and weight program, or (c) have given strong assurance that they plan to play this fall.

Be sure that *all* names are on the list providing coverage for every player. Check the spelling of each name to be sure it is accurate. Avoid using nicknames which might be difficult to identify by the insurance company.

Once the insurance list is prepared hold it until time for fall practice to start. Add or delete names at that time as needed. Be sure to keep a record of all names for your files.

Prepare Eligibility List

Most states require some type of eligibility list to be sent to the State High School Office indicating that all team members have met certain scholastic standards. This list can usually be compiled by checking the final grades of the players as recorded at the end of the previous school term (last May or June). Some players might be in summer school and not complete their eligibility requirements until late July or August. At any rate, go ahead and start the list, adding last-minute names if necessary. Carefully check the spelling of names, and be sure all players are listed. In some states inaccurate lists will cause the forfeiture of any games won while the inaccurate list was serving as the official statement of the school. Do not depend on the word of your players as to their scholastic record. Some players tend to forget what they passed and failed and do not understand the seriousness of the eligibility record. Be sure to consult *official school records* as you make your eligibility list.

Secure Physical Forms to Be Used in Player's Physical Exams

As you prepare for physical exams for your players be sure you have some type of official form for the doctor to check and then sign. Most state high school associations will provide standard forms upon request. If not, use a form like the one in Figure 7-1.

Be sure to reproduce enough forms for the maximum number of players who might be present later on for the physical exam.

Prepare Dressing Room for Start of Fall Practice

Here are some pointers for preparing the dressing room for the start of this fall's football practice. Begin now on this project, allowing yourself several weeks to complete the job:

● Start by taking everything possible out of the dressing room. This means items such as football equipment, benches, chairs, tables, etc.

● Remove all information from the bulletin board.

● Take down signs, slogans and pictures which are not permanently attached to the walls.

● Once the room has been cleared, clean it thoroughly (arrange for the school's summer custodial staff to help).

● Take some time to think of how the room could be better used. Do you have too many or too few benches for the players to

High School Physical Examination Form

Name of School _____School Year 19____ 19____

I certify that I have examined _____(name of student) and do/do not (strike out one) recommend him to be physically able to compete in interscholastic competition. These points were noted as follows:

Heart:

Before exercise _____
Immediately after exercise _____
After brief period _____
Blood pressure _____
Murmurs _____

Lungs:

Is there a history of
Chronic cough? _____
Sputum? _____
Other condition? _____

Weight in relation to height:

Underweight?_____
Overweight? _____
Satisfactory? _____

General Condition:

Excellent _____
Good _____
Fair _____
Poor _____

Signature of Examining Physician _____
Date _____

Figure 7-1

sit on? Can individual chairs (metal folding) for each player be provided? Should tables be moved to the other end of the locker room? Can lockers be shifted around to provide more space for each player? If your team has been winning, you might wish to leave things in the "traditional" way. If your team has not been doing well, a change in locker room appearance might give the players a "new look" attitude which can carry to the playing field.

● After arranging the basics (chairs, tables, etc.) of the room, add some paint to needed spots. In fact, you might wish to paint the entire room before refurnishing it. Every locker room should be painted in school colors! Put bare walls to use by painting mascots or school letters (example: "C" for Central High on them).

- Put up new bulletin board information. This includes schedules, scout reports of your first opponent, photos, general team information, or perhaps a football-related cartoon.
- Provide a separate bulletin board showing photos of current players who have maintained a certain scholastic average during the past year or school quarter. Many photos can be taken from last fall's football program if the players were on the team.
- Line the walls of the locker with photos of past teams, players who are now playing college football, or former coaches. Be sure to add individual photos of recent All-State (or other honored players). Make the locker room a place to enjoy as well as instilling a desire of each player to one day have his photo hanging permanently in the room.
- As calendars from area colleges arrive hang them in vacant spots around the room. We are speaking of the poster calendars featuring color photos that so many of the major colleges send to the high school coach during the late summer months.
- Try to think of several good slogans that fit this year's team. Paint them on boards (about 24″ × 24″ in size) and place them in easy to see spots around the room.
- Try to add at least one new item to the locker room. Perhaps a water cooler or a refrigerator from which cold drinks can be sold after practice could be obtained for the room. Some coaches like to pipe music into the dressing area.

The players deserve to return to fall practice and see that new ideas have been introduced. Hopefully, these ideas will inspire them to play better.

Have News Media Begin Announcing First Team Meeting or First Practice Dates

Since some teams will begin practice in early August, now is the time to review for the players and general public the dates of the first meetings and practices. Although players should have been given this information before school was out, some have probably forgotten it.

Write or call the news media in your area and ask them to announce the following information:

- The date of the physical exams.
- The date insurance money is to be turned in to the coach.
- The date and time to receive equipment.

- The date and time of the first team meeting.
- The *date* of the first practice session along with the *exact time* of practice.
- The date that team and individual photos will be taken.

If possible, have the media announce the information daily, or at least several times before the first meeting date.

Check Last Minute Details for
Football Camp in August

Some coaches take their football teams out of town during the first week or two of fall football practice (usually to a camp area or to a college campus) so that they can work without the distractions of home life. Other coaches chose to have a "football camp" at home with the players "living" at school (gym) during a week of concentrated drills. In either case, now is the time to complete final arrangements for camp.

- Check transportation arrangements to be sure that buses, vans, cars, or trucks are still available and in good repair.
- Check food arrangements to be sure that menus have been planned and time schedules for meals have been coordinated.
- Check room or sleeping arrangements. How will room keys be obtained? How many rooms are available?
- What areas are available for practice? Are indoor facilities available in case of rain?
- Will equipment such as two-man blocking sleds be taken to camp?
- Are there medical facilities nearby and how long will it take to get to them in case of emergency?
- How are financial arrangements to be handled?

These items have undoubtedly been arranged in advance, but a last-minute check might save some confusion later on.

Review Financial Situation for
Football Camp in August

Plans should have been made long ago to finance football camp. However, there are several things that could affect the total cost of camp. First, a change in prices relating to the use of football camp facilities may have taken place. A telephone call to those in authority at the camp location should be made. Second, there may be a change in the number of players and/or coaches who will attend camp. Several players may have moved over the summer months reducing the total number attending camp. On the other hand, some players may have been added to the roster.

One other thing to consider is how many "extras", such as providing soft drinks after each practice, will be needed.

Once all the financial facts are gathered review the total camp financial picture. Can you finance all you desire for your camp? Is there money to take additional players to camp? Must some players be dropped from the camp list due to lack of money? How many extras can be provided for the team? Hopefully, enough money will be available to provide for an excellent camp.

Contact Statistician and Discuss
Plans for the Season

If your statistician from last season will be returning, contact him and arrange a time to review exactly what you want him to do concerning keeping football statistics. Use the mimeographed statistic sheets which you prepared last month (see Chapter 6—June). Discuss any changes that are to be made. Provide him with a season schedule so that he can plan to have those dates open on his calendar. Discuss travel or meals with the team that might include the statistician. Talk about any financial arrangements if the statistician is to be paid.

If you have to use a statistician who has not done the job before, review the previously mentioned items with him and make a detailed study of the stat sheet. You might even let him watch an old film and practice taking stats from the film. Do not run the film in slow motion or allow him to back the film up and show a replay. Make him realize that each play must be followed closely and watched carefully, knowing at all times exactly what he is looking for.

Order Special Buses or Transportation
for This Fall's Games

If your teams owns its own bus, you have no problem here. But if you will need transportation to out-of-town games or even to getting across town to your own stadium, place your bus order at this time. Contact several companies that have charter bus service. Secure their rates and make sure which companies can provide the type of bus (large or small) that you will need on the date that you need it.

Once you have decided on which bus service to use, get your dates and rates put in writing. If the company has no forms, use one similar to the one in Figure 7-2.

Transportation Form

Name of Company ————————————————Telephone ———————————
Name of Agent ———————————————————————————————————————
Company Address ——————————————————————————————————————
School ————————————————High School Telephone ———————————
School Address ———————————————————————————————————————
Coach ——
Type of bus(es) needed —————————————————————————————————
Number of buses needed ——————————————
Date needed————————————————— 19——
Time bus(es) should be at school ————————
Destination ——
Estimated time of return ——————————————————————————————
Stops made along the way (for meals, etc.)——————————————————
Number of people riding the bus(es) ———————————————————————
Rate charged ———————————————————————————————————————
How will payment be made? ————————————————————————————
When will payment be made? ————————————————————————————
Signature of Bus Company Official ——————————————————————————
Signature of School Official ———————————————————————————————

Figure 7-2

Be sure to make carbon copies of the transportation form, giving one to the company and one to your school principal. Keep a copy for your records.

Final Check on any Equipment
That Was Ordered, but Not Yet Delivered

Chapter 1—January recommended that many items be ordered in that month to insure their arrival in plenty of time for the start of the fall football season. Most of these items should be in your possession now. Check carefully to be sure that all ordered items have arrived. If you find that some equipment has not been delivered, send a letter, or better yet, call the vendor. Remind him that you need your equipment immediately to be prepared for the start of practice in a few weeks. In case some of the items ordered cannot be supplied by the time you need them, you still have time to cancel the order and possibly secure the items elsewhere.

Secure Bids on Medical Supplies

Although other football-related items are ordered earlier in the year, we like to wait until just before the start of the season to order medical supplies. This insures their being fresh and also provides an opportunity to purchase the latest ideas in training and medical supplies. Secure bids from several vendors. Be sure the company you deal with can furnish the amount of supplies you will need. Here is a checklist of medical supplies:

— Abrasion Ointment
— Alcohol Rub
— Ammonia Caps
— Ankle Wrap
— Aspirin
— Air Splints
— Applicators, 6″ with cotton tip
— Balm
— Ball Cleaner
— Bandage Scissors
— Cold Packs
— Cold Spray
— Cotton
— Cotton Applicators
— Dextrose Tablets
— Eyeglass Holder
— Elastic Bandages
— Firm Grip
— Foam Rubber
— Foot and Body Powder
— Fungal Foot Spray
— Germicide Spray
— Gauze Pads (2×2, 3×3, 4×4)
— Heel Cups
— Hot Packs

— Insect Repellent Spray
— Jock Itch Powder
— Knee and Ankle Braces
— Liniment
— Massage Lotion
— Mouthwash
— Petroleum Jelly
— Rosin Bags
— Salt Tablets
— Scissors
— Splint Kit
— Shower Soap
— Supports (Ankle, Knee, Elbow)
— Tablet Dispenser
— Tongue Depressors
— Tape Cutter
— Tape Cutter Replacement Blades
— Trainer's Travel Kit
— Trainer's Manual
— Trainer's Tables
— Taping Table
— Vitamin C Tablets
— Whistle Tip Cover

Make Sure Stadium Repairs Have Been Made

It was recommended in Chapter 5—May that a list of stadium repairs be presented to school officials so that the stadium would be in excellent shape for the opening of the fall season. Hopefully, these repairs have been made. If you made a stadium repair list like the one in Figure 5-1, refer to it to be sure that all work has been completed. Give reminder notices to school officials or to the workers themselves concerning work that has not been completed. Remind them that the season is fast approaching, but that several weeks remain to finish the work. Give yourself a note to check every few days to be sure needed repairs are being completed.

Check Field Line Marking Machine

Make sure that any machinery needed to mark off the game field or practice field is in good working order. Also be sure that the machine is where you left it at the end of last season (or spring practice). Track or baseball teams might have used the machine during the spring, so don't assume that you know where it is. Also, don't assume that it is in good working order. It may have been abused since you last used it. There is still time for minor repairs before the season starts if you act now.

Compile List of Phone Numbers
That Will be Used During the Coming Season

Once the football season starts, you will be too busy to stop and look up every telephone number that you need to call. Solve the problem by looking these numbers up now when you have some leisure time. Compile the list of numbers and post them on the wall near your office phone. Make a copy for the phone at the stadium as well as a copy for your home phone. Here are some suggestions of numbers to list:

- School Principal
- School Superintendent
- Board of Education Members
- School Custodian
- School Maintenance Workers and Repairmen
- Ambulance Service
- Hospital
- Team Doctors
- Assistant Coaches
- Junior High Coaches
- Junior High School Principal
- Coaches Offices of each team on your schedule
- Coaches Offices of each team in your area or region
- State High School Office
- Officials Association (referees, etc)
- Colleges that recruit in your area

- Newspaper Sports Department
- Radio Stations
- TV Stations
- Touchdown Club or Booster Club President
- Band Director
- Cheerleader Sponsor
- Cheerleaders (at least the cheerleader captain)
- All Football Team Members
- Team Managers and Trainers
- Photographer (for still pictures)
- Camera Man for Game Films
- Film Distributors and Film Developers
- Bus and Other Transportation Services
- Restaurants (for pre- and post-game meals)
- Local Recreation Department
- Police Department
- Fire Department
- Statistician
- Sporting Goods Dealers
- Trophy Dealers
- Printing Company (for football programs, etc)
- Stadium Press Box

Prepare and Mail College Prospect List to Colleges

Perhaps many colleges sent prospect information cards to you last spring and this summer. It is good to fill them out and return them. However, if you have one or several college prospects for whom you might wish to prepare more detailed information, mimeograph a number of copies, and send it to the colleges in your area. A sample prospect list is shown in Figure 7-3.

Enclose a photo with the list. Add any other information that would give a good description of your player. But be careful not to go overboard. If you have a real prospect, the colleges will find him. Just give them some basic information and make films available should they request them.

COLLEGE PROSPECT LIST
19____

(Name of your school) _____
(School Address) _____
(School Phone) _____ (Office Phone) _____
(Head Coach) _____

MIKE HERNDON:
    Class—senior in 19____
    Scholastic ability—Has "B" average
    Height—6'3"
    Weight—231 lbs.
    Age—17 Birthday—_____ 19____
    Address _____
    Parents—Mr. and Mrs. Jack Herndon
    Offensive position—Has started at both center and tackle. Will play
       mostly at tackle during senior year.
    Defensive position—Tackle
    Honors: All City as junior
    40 yd. dash—Not timed
    Character—Has excellent character. Is the hardest worker on squad. Is
       the type of player who does things right without being told more than
       once.
    Other sports—Wrestling. Mike finished 4th in the state (AAAA schools)
       wrestling tournament.

Figure 7-3

Plan Daily Schedule to Be Used
At Football Camp in August

If you plan to go to camp in August, now is the time to prepare your daily schedule. You will be with your players 24 hours a day and need careful preparation. Ask the help of your staff members. Use the things that you liked about last year's camp. Eliminate those things that you didn't like. A sample daily football camp schedule is shown in Figure 7-4 on page 106.

Plan for Locker Room Security

Be sure your locker room is safe for your players to leave their personal belongings such as watches, rings, billfolds, etc. during practice. The best solution is to have individual lockers secured by key or combination locks. We prefer combination locks because

CAMP SCHEDULE FOR 3RD DAY OF CAMP
Wednesday

6:30 a.m.	Awake
6:45 a.m.	Exercise in front of dormitory—Coach _____ in charge
7:00 a.m.	Jog one mile
7:30 a.m.	Breakfast
8:30 a.m.	Taping
8:45 a.m.	Quarterback meeting with Coach _____
9:00 a.m.	Practice
10:30 a.m.	End practice
11:30 a.m.	Special teams (kicking) meeting
12:00 noon	Lunch
1:30 p.m.	Offensive line meeting with Coach _____
	Defensive backs meeting with Coach _____
2:00 p.m.	Swimming pool for those who desire—Coaches _____
	and _____ in charge
3:30 p.m.	Taping
3:45 p.m.	Special teams practice
4:45 p.m.	End special teams practice
5:30 p.m.	Dinner
6:30 p.m.	Defensive Signal callers meeting with Coach _____
6:45 p.m.	Taping
7:00 p.m.	Practice
8:30 p.m.	End practice
9:00 p.m.	Recreation room
10:00 p.m.	Team devotionals
10:30 p.m.	Soft drinks and snacks
11:00 p.m.	Lights out

Figure 7-4

this eliminates the problem of what to do with the key during practice. If your players use combination locks, be sure to copy down the combination and keep it in the office. This allows the coach to get into the locker in case a player is injured and must be taken to the hospital and needs personal items. If the players must supply their own locks for their lockers, it is a good idea not to issue a locker until the player provides a lock. This encourages the player to have his lock on the first day of practice and also insures that no items will be "stolen" from an unprotected locker. If your school can afford it, purchase 50-100 locks and rent or issue them to your players.

If your locker room does not have individual lockers, instruct a manager to collect the players' valuables in a bag. Then lock the bag in the coaches' office or some other safe place until after practice. Also, remind the players that they should not come to practice with a lot of money, unnecessary watches or rings, etc.

Prepare a Set of Keys to All Football Rooms
for Each Coach

Start by making a list of all your assistant football coaches. Look over the list and decide which ones will need keys. Some assistants will need a full set of keys to all doors in case you (the head coach) are not around all the time. Some coaches will need keys to certain doors only, such as the junior varsity coach needing a key to his locker room, or a trainer needing a key to get to the medical supplies.

Be sure to give a set of keys to the school principal, and perhaps a set to the custodian who cleans up. Always remember to ask assistants to immediately report any lost keys. Think twice before issuing any keys to student managers. As good as your manager may be, he is still a student. Once a key is lost or in the wrong hands, you cannot safely control your equipment.

If you have more than 4 or 5 football locker room keys (separate keys for your office, equipment room, training room, etc), identify them quickly by spray-painting them each a different color. Or if you have a metal-stamping kit, mark each key by number (1, 2, 3) or by initials (CO for Coaches Office, TR for Training Room, EQ. R for Equipment Room).

8

Check to Be Sure Each Player Has Had a Physical Exam

By August every player on your varsity and junior varsity team should have had a physical exam by a qualified doctor. No player should be allowed to practice or play in a game until he has had this exam. Most teams will set aside a certain day or night and have the team doctor come to the school and give the exams. Some players may get a physical from their own family doctor.

There are usually several team members who fail to get their exam by the start of practice due to vacations, etc. Use a chart like the one in Figure 8-1 to keep an accurate list of each player and his physical exam status.

PHYSICAL EXAM CHECKLIST

Name of Player	Name of Doctor	Date Examined	Passed: Yes	No	Comment
1._____	_____	___19__	____	____	_____
2._____	_____	___19__	____	____	_____
3._____	_____	___19__	____	____	_____
4._____	_____	___19__	____	____	_____
5._____	_____	___19__	____	____	_____

Figure 8-1

It is a good idea to keep these checklists for several years in case a question arises as to the physical condition of a player.

Check to Be Sure Each Player Has Proper Insurance

As you prepare the insurance list to send in to the company, *double-check* the names on the list. Do not assume that all names have been included. Check the list against the team roster. Better still, gather the team together before the start of the first practice and read each name aloud, asking each player to answer. Any players not called from the insurance list can then be added. Be careful to check for any players who might be *absent* as well as *not on the insurance list*.

Some schools allow players who have adequate insurance at home (a parent has insurance with his place of employment) to get a signed statement releasing the school and the coaches from responsibility of payment in case of injury. Such a statement should resemble the one in Figure 8-2. Be sure school officials agree with the legality of the statement before using it.

If some players use these forms, be sure to file them carefully so that they can be easily and quickly located when needed.

HOME INSURANCE FORM

We hereby release _____High School, its coaches, school officials, and Board of Education from any responsibility for payment of hospital or doctor bills in connection with any injury suffered by our son _____(name) while engaging in practice or games during the 19____ season. We have adequate insurance to cover our son. Our policy is with _____ (name of insurance company). The policy number is _____ . Our local agent, or person to contact if needed, is _____ .

(Parent or guardian) _____
(Home Phone) _____
(Date signed) _____ 19____

Figure 8-2

Have Each Player Sign a Doctor Release Form

There have been cases where an injured football player has been taken to a hospital or doctor's office, but has not been given immediate treatment due to lack of parental consent. Figure 8-3 is what we call a Doctor Release Form. It simply gives parental consent for any doctor or hospital official to take whatever action is necessary to treat their injured son.

DOCTOR RELEASE FORM

As parents (guardian) of _____(name of player) of _____ High School we hereby give our consent for the coaches or school officials of _____ High School to take our son for treatment at the best available hospital or doctor's office in case he is injured. We further give consent for the hospital officials or the doctor in charge to take any action necessary to provide the best treatment for our son until such time as we are in contact with the medical officials.

(Parent or guardian) _____
(Home Phone) _____
(Work Phone) _____
(Date) _____ 19____

Figure 8-3

The most important thing to remember about having the Doctor Release Forms is that they must be available immediately when needed. Have each player fill one out complete with his parent's signature. File them alphabetically and put them in a small portable folder. Put the folder in a convenient place such as the coaches' office or training room. As soon as any player is injured pick up the entire folder and take it to the hospital or doctor's office in case the player's form is needed. *Be sure to take the folder with you when playing out of town games*, especially if the parents of some of the players will not be attending the game.

Prepare Insurance Folder

Keep a neat, organized folder containing all information dealing with football insurance. Put the following items in the folder:

- Team insurance list
- Additions to the list (players who might have joined the team late and were recently added to the list)
- Deletions (names taken off the list due to a player's dropping off the team)
- Claim forms (to be used when a player files a claim)
- All letters and correspondence with the insurance company
- Names and addresses and phone numbers of the insurance agents you deal with

- A copy of the terms of the football insurance policy
- A record of past claims (for reference)

Be sure that all coaches are familiar with the folder and can handle insurance matters in your absence.

Order Film

Wait until this month to order the film which will be used for your game films. This insures that the film will be as new as possible. You might need to shop around and get the best bid price before ordering. Try to make an accurate estimate of the amount of film you will need so that none will be left over at the end of the season. Your camera man should be able to help you with this. Once you have received your film keep it in a cool place. Notify your camera man that the film has arrived so that he can pick up what he needs and can be ready to give a good picture of your first game.

Try On Game Uniforms and
Number Each Player's Game Pants

Once you have started fall practice and have a good idea of the players on your team, take time at the end of a practice to fit each player with his game uniform. Jerseys will not be too much of a problem unless an unusually small player is issued an unusually large jersey. Pants are a different story. Players like them to fit perfectly!

As you hand out game pants to try on, make sure those who will do most of the playing get at the first of the line. Give them a pair of pants as near their size as possible. Make the player put the pants on. Do not let him assume that they will fit. For as sure as you do, this player will approach you on opening game night, when your mind is on one thousand things, and request a change of pants. Tell the players that you will stay as long as they like in order to get the proper fit for their pants, but after today do not make a request to change. Once a player has made his selection and is satisfied write his jersey number in the *back inside* of the pants with a laundry marker (or some other marker that will not wash out). Put the game pants back on the shelf, then issue them quickly by number on game day.

Turn In Program Ads, Photos,
and Your Roster to Printer

In Chapter 4—April, it was suggested that the football program be planned and a printer be selected. It was also recommended that some groups (cheerleaders, players, Booster Club members) begin selling advertisements for the program. Call the printer and make an appointment with him. Take him all advertisement material plus a copy of your team roster. Photos, if not yet taken, can be added just before printing, but the printer should be given an idea of the number and size of the photos that you want in the program. The printer will probably ask you to approve the layout of the program, and to proofread the material for errors just before printing. Set up a time to do this, building the time around your practice schedule.

Write Opponents for Copies of Their Rosters
for the Programs

Write letters to, or call, each opponent on your *home* schedule. Request that they send a team roster as soon as possible for the football program. Explain that the printer needs the roster so that the programs can be produced and returned to the school before the beginning of the season. You must realize that some coaches do not determine their final varsity roster until a week or two before the opening of the season, therefore, providing an early roster is impossible. In some cases you must make back-up phone calls, or write second or even third letters, in order to receive the roster. But keep trying. The program is not worth much without this information. Once you receive some rosters, rush them to your printer. He can run those programs now, and, hopefully the last one will arrive before the deadline.

Check with Band Concerning Pre-game Plans
and Out-of-Town Trips

Your school's band program can be a valuable asset to your football program if you will show some concern for their needs. Call a meeting with your band director, and possibly even your school principal. Ask the band director to outline what he would like to do at the games. Here are some questions that might be asked and discussed:

1. Would he like to do a pre-game show?
2. If so, explain to him *your* pre-game warm-up schedule (on the field) and see if his schedule conflicts.
3. Does he understand that the pre-game show must be completed by a certain time?
4. What type of half time activities are planned by the band?
5. Will the visiting school bring its band?
6. If so, will they perform at half time also?
7. Does he understand that the half time show must be completed within a definite period of time or a penalty will be called.
8. Does the band expect any athletic department help in planning out-of-town trips? If so, what type of help—financial, transportation, meals?

It is very important that all channels of communication remain open from the football team to the band or any other similar school group. Show concern for them and their problems and you'll develop some loyal backing.

Pre-season Meeting with Cheerleaders and Sponsor

Several weeks before the first game invite the cheerleaders and their sponsor to come to your office and discuss their plans for the season. Inquire if all the supplies they ordered have arrived, such as megaphones, pom-poms, spirit ribbons, buttons, etc. Talk with them about their plans for the first pep rally and ask what the football team and coaches can do to make it a success. Discuss their plans for travel to out-of-town games, as well as meals they will eat with the team during the season.

In Chapter 5—May, it was recommended that the cheerleaders be allowed to have a separate bulletin board in the football locker room, or perhaps in the hallway outside the locker room. This could be used for messages to the players about pep rallies or any other items of player/cheerleader interest. If you OK this idea, now is the time to let them get started on this project.

Be sure the sponsor is given schedules of games, including starting times, team rosters, and any other information that will make them feel a part of your program.

Send in Eligibility Report

In most states all schools have to send in reports to the state office which controls high school athletics concerning the number of subjects each player passed during the most recent quarter or semester of school. Check the names of these players carefully. Have your school principal or counselor double-check your work to make sure no errors have been made. Be sure the reports are sent in on time. Call your roll before practice one day by reading the names on the eligibility report. This is a check to be sure all player's names on the report have been sent in.

Mimeograph Football Camp Checklist
and Information Sheet for Each Player and Coach

If you take your football team out of town for several days or perhaps for a week of pre-season work you need to give each player a detailed itinerary plus checklists of things to take. Provide copies for coaches and team managers as well as trainers and any other personnel making the trip. Be sure to leave copies for your school officials (principal, for example). This is merely to keep them informed.

Since many pre-season football workout locations are on a college campus or on a leased campsite (see Chapter 7—July) it is a good idea to call someone at the camp location and ask about special rules pertaining to the area. These will need to be included in the camp information to players. Ask also about emergency telephone numbers, hospital numbers and addresses, etc.

Figure 8-4 shows an example of a football camp itinerary and checklist. It might give you some ideas of what you want to include in your itinerary. (See page 115.)

Be sure to save several copies of the itinerary for next season's camp.

Review Medical Emergency Procedures
with Coaching Staff

Before you step on the field for your first practice, gather all of your coaches (junior varsity included) together and go over the details of what to do in case of an emergency. Start by reviewing

ITINERARY AND CHECKLIST

Football Camp   Central High School   Macon, Georgia
19___

Sunday, August 14—2:00 p.m. to 3:00 p.m.
1. All players report to the gym.
2. Bring *one* suitcase per player (no clothes on hangers).
3. Load suitcase on the bus or truck. A coach will assist you.
4. You or your roommate should bring a small fan. Load this on the bus or truck also.
5. Pack all football equipment and load on the bus or truck. (See football checklist on another sheet.)
6. Bring $15 cash (no checks, please) as part of the camp expenses. The Touchdown Club will pay the rest for you.

Monday, August 15—6:45 a.m.
1. Be at the gym no later than 6:45 a.m. The bus will leave at 7:00 a.m. for the four-hour trip to Rome, Georgia. Make your travel arrangements so that you will be sure to be at the gym by 6:45 a.m. We will not have time to wait or to telephone those who are late.
2. Bring any last-minute items that could not be packed on Sunday such as toothbrush or pillow. Keep these items with you in your seat on the bus.
3. We will take a 15-minute break in Atlanta at about 8:30 a.m. Coaches will provide a light snack.
4. We will arrive in Rome about 11:00 a.m. and go directly to the college campus where we will check in and prepare for lunch at 12:00 noon.
5. After lunch we will go to our dormitory, unpack, and be ready for a 4:00 p.m. practice.

Friday, August 19
1. Pack after the morning practice and prepare for the noon meal.
2. After lunch pack your equipment and suitcase on the equipment bus or truck.
3. We hope to leave campus at 2:00 p.m.
4. We will stop in Atlanta at _____ Stadium which is the site of our first road game this fall. We have received permission to work out at the stadium from 3:30 p.m. to 5:00 p.m.
5. Leave at 5:15 p.m. for Macon. We hope to arrive home at about 6:45-7:00 p.m.

General Information to Players and Parents

1. We will hold football camp at _____ College in Rome, Georgia, about 65 miles northwest of Atlanta.
2. Approximately 65 players, coaches, managers and trainers will attend.
3. Players will be housed in a college dormitory, two to a room.
4. Mail, if sent early in the week, will be received by the player at this address: (Fill in address here).
5. In case of emergency call this number: (Fill in here) This is the phone number of the college director in charge of visiting groups. He will pass on any messages or information to Coach _____ who will act in accordance with the emergency.

6. We expect every player to act and dress as a representative of Central High School. Keep neat and clean-shaven.
7. Players are not to go to any other dormitory or to leave our campus area for any reason. Any player who violates this rule will be sent home.
8. Do not invite friends to visit the campus while we are there. No person other than our players, coaches, etc. is allowed in our dormitory. Do not ask friends to call our dormitory and ask to speak to you.
9. Any damage done by a player to any campus property will be paid for by the player.
10. Play radios low to avoid disturbing others.
11. Players will not need to take much money to camp. $5-$10 for soft drinks and incidentals will be adequate.
12. Be careful not to lose your room key. If the key has a hole in it, tie it to your shoelace.
13. All players must report for every meal—no exceptions!
14. The college requests that we observe these rules:
    - use walkwaxs instead of walking on the grass
    - no fishing or swimming in the lake
    - do not take food or drink out of the cafeteria
15. There is an indoor swimming pool and a recreation center which we will be able to use at certain times. Swimming will be only at designated times and with *three* coaches present!!!
16. Campus officials comment each year on the good behavior of our team. We intend them to be able to make the same comment after this year!

CHECKLIST OF PERSONAL ITEMS
TO TAKE TO CAMP

(*Suggestion:* after using this checklist to pack for the trip to Rome, put it in your suitcase and check the items again as you pack for the trip home.)

_____ sheets
_____ pillow
_____ light blanket (if desired)
_____ one pair of long pants
_____ shirts
_____ socks
_____ shoes
_____ underclothes
_____ light jacket (if desired)
_____ shorts
_____ toothpaste and toothbrush
_____ razor and lather
_____ soap
_____ comb or brush
_____ towels
_____ washcloth
_____ small fan or radio (if desired)
_____ tennis shoes (for practice in gym in case of rain)
_____ belt
_____ paper, pen, stamps, envelope (if desired)
_____ pajamas

_____ special medicine or vitamins (Parent: please contact Coach
_____ if any special medicine is to be taken by your son)
_____ swim suit (if desired)
_____ other
_____ other

Football Equipment Packing List

_____ helmet
_____ chin strap
_____ mouthpiece
_____ practice jersey
_____ shoulder pads (make sure all strings and straps are OK)
_____ pants
_____ belt
_____ girdle hip pads
_____ knee pads
_____ thigh pads
_____ shoes (take two pairs if you have them)
_____ white practice socks (several pairs)
_____ special pads (if any)
_____ supporters
_____ white practice shorts
_____ T-shirts
_____ sweatbands (if desired)
_____ other

Note to players: You are responsible for double-checking to be sure you have every piece of your equipment. Although the managers will take some extra items, things like helmets or shoes will be very difficult to fit in case you leave yours. Pack with a partner. Each of you check the others equipment!!!

Figure 8-4

the medical kit items. Let each coach see what is in the kit. Discuss where the kit will be kept during practice. If the varsity and junior varsity practice on separate fields near each other, keep the kit between the two. If their fields are far apart, provide two kits.

Be sure to review how to use each item in the medical kit. Know what members of the staff are qualified to give CPR. Remind each coach that the ambulance, hospital and team doctor's telephone numbers are (or should be) posted near the office phone. Stress that when taking a player to the hospital or doctor's office be sure to take the player's _Doctor Release Form_ and the _Insurance Folder_ (see page 110 in this chapter) with him. And finally, tell the coaches not to forget to contact an injured boy's parents as soon as possible.

Order Medical Kit and Training Supplies

In Chapter 7—July, we mentioned getting bids on medical supplies. Now that fall practice is ready to begin select the best prices and place your order. Your supplies are sure to be fresh and up to date. It is a good idea to consider getting medical supplies locally if possible. You will become familiar with what the local dealer stocks and can quickly pick up additional supplies as needed.

If you don't have a trainer, appoint one of your assistant coaches to be in charge of these supplies. Make sure players or student managers aren't handing out medical supplies to themselves or other players.

Plan for Liquid Consumption During and After Practice

The early fall practices will be held in warm to hot weather depending on your location in the United States. Here are some ideas for providing liquids for the players:

1. Water may be available from nearby fountains, or can be taken to the field in containers.
2. Ice can be taken to the field in almost any type of container.
3. Soft drinks can be purchased by players or by the school.
4. Commercially prepared liquid, designed to prevent dehydration, can be used.
5. Check with some local merchants who serve orange, grape, etc. drinks in their restaurants or fast food stores. If they are team fans, they may be willing to contribute some orange or grape concentrate, providing plenty of liquids before and after practice.

You might also wish to ask cheerleaders to be present at certain times during your practice to aid in pouring and serving liquids to the players.

Have Pre-season Financial Meeting with Principal and Business Manager

The budget for the coming school year should have already been planned (see Chapter 6—June). Meet with your principal and business manager to discuss items such as these:

- Will the game photographer be paid after each game or at the end of the season?
- Should the laundry bill (game uniforms) be paid by the week, or month, or at the end of the season?
- How many charter buses will be needed for out-of-town games and how will they be paid?
- How should payment for the first pre-game and/or post-game meal be made? To whom should the check be written?
- Does the coach need some cash on hand for small items such as bulbs for the projector, or stamps?
- Has all ad money been collected from businesses that placed advertisements in the football program?

Set up a schedule to meet on a regular basis to talk about finances with the principal and business manager. It can help keep everyone informed as to the financial condition of the football team in particular and the athletic department in general.

Send Roster to Opposing Teams

As soon as you are sure of your varsity roster make copies to send to your opponents (especially out-of-town opponents). You have probably received rosters from some schools which did not contain enough information. Consider these things for your team's roster:

- Player's name
- Jersey number (If the numbers on your light and dark sets of jerseys don't all match be sure to include two columns, one of light jersey numbers and the other for the dark jersey numbers.)
- Offensive position
- Defensive position (you might choose to use a separate column for defensive positions)
- Height
- Weight
- Class in school (soph, junior, senior)
- Parent's name (optional)
- Major subject in school (not usually done in high school)

Be sure to include this additional information on the page:

- The name of your school and its location

- School colors
- Team nickname or mascot
- Coaches names
- Name of school principal and/or superintendent
- Team managers
- Team doctors
- Band director
- Cheerleaders and cheerleader sponsor
- School enrollment
- Region or league that team is a member of
- Statistician
- Team photographer

Send Roster and Team Information to News Media

Compile a list of all the newspapers, radio stations, television stations, and other news media organizations in your area. Mimeograph your information and make each a booklet about your team and the coming season. Here are some examples of what to put in the booklet:

Front Page—Put your team name, and the calendar year. Dress it up with a drawing of your mascot. Or you might want to print your schedule, leaving plenty of space between each team to put a small drawing of each opponent's mascot (an Indian, or Bulldog, etc.).

Page One—Put a copy of your roster.

Page Two—Show the depth chart of your offensive team.

Page Three—Show the depth chart of your specialists—punters, place kickers, holders, snappers, passers, etc.

Page Four—Show your defensive depth chart.

Page Five—List your team records during the past ten (or more) years. Indicate championships won.

Page Six—Show your team statistics from last season.

Page Seven—Give your junior varsity schedule and show their results from last season's games.

Page Eight—List the telephone number of your office and home, plus numbers of each assistant coach's home phones.

Page Nine—List each team in your region or league. Give the name of each team's coach, the team nickname or mascot, school colors, and season schedule of games.

Page Ten—Sketch a map showing every team in your region or league, or every team on your schedule. This will show the relationship of each school as to location. Write in the miles between each school. This map will enable the reader to see at a glance that "_____ High is 35 miles southwest of _____ High".

Page Eleven—General information such as: names of cheerleaders (if not on page one roster), band information, press parking at the stadium information, names of Board of Education members, etc.

Page Twelve—(use more pages if needed) Give a brief description of each football coach on the staff. Tell where he went to high school, teams he was on there, honors won while in high school, where he went to college and teams he was on there, coaching experience, plus something about his family.

After finishing the booklets deliver them personally or mail them to all media personnel. You might also want to send a copy to media people in your opponent's towns.

Have Principal Plan for Substitute Teachers When Football Coaches Will Be Gone on Trips

If you will have to leave school early several times this fall for football trips, someone is going to have to substitute for you. Let your principal know now the dates that you (and your staff) will have to leave early, and the exact hour that you plan to leave your class. This will give him plenty of time to have a substitute available so that he will not have to assign your classes to another teacher during a free (or planning) period.

Check Stadium Lights

It is quite possible your stadium lights have not been turned on since last fall. Check them out late one evening after practice (or hold a night practice). Have a member of the local power company (or whoever might be in charge of repairing the lights) present. Arrange to replace bulbs as needed. Don't forget to check the lights in the dressing rooms, the concession stands, the ticket booths, and the rest rooms. Be sure proper lighting is available in the press box, and along the poles in the parking area.

Check Scoreboard

Connect your scoreboard controls. Flip the switches showing every number on the board. Notice where bulbs need replacing. Set the clock and time it with an accurate watch to be sure it is not too fast or too slow. Make repairs immediately as the season will start within a few weeks. If you have a special operator of your scoreboard at each of your games, take him with you as you check the controls. This will help him understand any problems you might be having. Just as a final safety measure, check the scoreboard one last time a day or two before the first home game. If any last-minute problems have developed you still may have time to make corrections.

Check Material to Line Field

Several weeks before your first game check your supply room for the following things:

1. Marble dust or other material such as the "liquid" used to "paint" lines on the field
2. Line marking machine (be sure it is in good repair)
3. One or several long strings (heavy-type cord)
4. Stakes to secure the string
5. Wheelbarrow or small wagon to carry the marble dust

You might want to use these materials to mark the practice field. You definitely will need them as your first home game approaches.

Pre-season Check with Film Processor

Talk in person or by phone with the people who will process your game films. Tell them how you plan to get the game film to them after each game (will coaches bring it? must it be sent by bus, or mail?). Ask when you might expect the film to be ready (this will vary with home and road games). Be sure you know where to pick it up (at the location of the film processor? at the bus station?). Be sure the processor has your schedule (point out if some games are played on Saturday night instead of the regular Friday dates). Exchange phone numbers so that communication will be good at all times (such as immediately after a game).

Pre-season Check with Cameraman

In Chapter 5—May, we reviewed a list of items to check with your cameraman in preparation for this season. Give him a call, now that the season is upon you, and double-check your plans. It is also a good idea to talk about possible back-up plans in case he gets sick, etc. during the season and will need a stand-in. Suggest that he always take a friend along with him who can begin to learn how to operate the camera. Ask the friend to be ready to take over in case of emergency.

Prepare Scout Assignment Sheet

It is important that your scouts have some advance notice of the games you want them to scout. Start by locating schedules of each of your opponents (some state high school associations provide a master schedule of all schools).

Study the schedules carefully to determine whom you will need to scout. In some cases two teams on your schedule will be playing each other providing an opportunity to scout both at the same time. Determine how many scouts you have available each weekend. This will vary because you might play on Friday and an opponent you want to scout plays on Saturday. This will allow you or a varsity assistant to scout this game without relying on your regular scouts (usually junior varsity coaches). After compiling your information put it on a form (see Figure 8-5) and distribute it (mimeographed copies) to all scouts.

SCOUT ASSIGNMENT SHEET

Date	We Play	Team Scouted	Their Opponent	At	Scouts
Sept. 1	Washington	Douglass	Northeast	Atlanta	Sanders L. Hill
Sept. 2 (Sat)	———	Columbus	Griffin	Griffin	Bowers Plagge
Sept. 8	Columbus	Warner Robins	Lee	Warner R.	L. Hill
Sept. 15	Douglass	Richmond Academy	Savannah	Savannah	Bowers Sanders
Sept. 22	Warner Robins—No other games being played in the area No scouting assignments				

Figure 8-5

Note: It is important to list whom *we play* since it gives the scouts a reference point as to where we are in the schedule.

We also give each scout a mimeographed list containing the following information:

SCOUTING NOTES

1. Keep ahead of the scout schedule. Know when your time comes to scout.
2. If you have a serious conflict let the head coach know immediately so that changes in the schedule can be made.
3. We will provide $_____ for an out-of-town trip up to ____ miles, and $_____ for a trip over ____ miles.
4. Be sure to pick up a scout form (see Chapter 6—June) from the football office before you leave to scout.
5. Return the completed scout form to the head coach by noon the following day.

Pre-season Check with Officials for Games

Make a last-minute check with the officials who will work your first home game. Review directions to your stadium, and find out when to expect them so that you can have someone at the stadium to watch for them. Give them directions to the room or area where they are to dress. Determine if they will need shower facilities, towels, soap, etc. Be sure to agree on whether the officials will be paid after the game, or if a check will be sent to their association later.

Contact Ticket Takers, Security, etc.

Many of these people are probably the same ones who worked last season for you and should be familiar with their jobs. Contact those *in charge* of the ticket takers and security. Double-check the number of people you will need (this will probably vary from game to game depending on your estimate of the crowd). Be sure to show the security people exactly where you want them. For example, you may assign two for the parking lot, one near the band or cheerleaders, three on the home side, and two on the visiting side.

Final Check with Chain Holders

Call those people who will handle your down marker and yardage chains during the game. Be sure they are aware of your opening home date. Tell them what time to be at the stadium. Explain that you have checked the down marker and chains (see Chapter 5—May) and that they are in good repair. Remind them of where the chains and down marker will be stored (so that the holders won't look you up during an important pre-game meeting and ask where they are). If any pay is involved, be sure to agree on when the payment will be made and how much money you will need to pay them.

Clean and Check Press Box at Stadium

Several days before your first home game prepare your press box to receive writers, radio personnel, and scouts. Here is a checklist:

1. Sweep and dust the entire area.
2. Be sure the lights in the press box work.
3. Provide an ample number of chairs.
4. Add useful items, such as a pencil sharpener.
5. Be sure there is electrical power in the wall sockets.
6. Test the public address system controls.
7. Clean windows (if any).
8. Check the telephone and have a telephone book handy.
9. Label certain areas for *radio announcers, local newspaper reporters,* and *visiting scouts.*
10. Be sure to have an *Authorized Personnel Only* sign on the door.

Select and Purchase Game Balls

Several weeks before your first game talk with your sporting goods dealers about game balls. Find out what might be new on the market. Select one or two of your favorite brands of balls. Use each at practice and allow your quarterback and receivers, plus those involved in the kicking game to test the different balls. Purchase several of the most popular brand. Some quarterbacks like to start the game with a new ball. Others like to use a ball that has been slightly used. At any rate, be sure those who will use the ball (QB, receivers, kickers, snappers) make the ball decision, not the coach.

Make Laundry Arrangements for Game Uniforms

Some schools have their own laundry facilities. This is good unless the uniforms get so dirty that professional laundry service is needed. Call several local laundries and ask about price and the time that would be needed to clean your uniforms. If you will use professional laundry service each week, ask about pick up and delivery service. You might even need to send a schedule (if you will handle laundry after each game) with written notes detailing when to pick up the laundry and when you need it back. Stress the urgency of having your uniforms returned to you on time!

Final Check of Junior Varsity Game Officials, Chain Crews, etc.

Although you have taken great care to insure having officials and chain crews for your varsity games, this task is often overlooked for your junior varsity games until the last minute. The best solution is to instruct your JV coaches to be responsible for this job. Provide them with phone numbers of the people involved so that they can make their own last-minute checks. Give them a written reminder several weeks before their first home game. Double-check with them several days before the game. Be sure to provide them with information concerning finances (officials' pay, travel), places to dress, etc. just as you have planned to do with your varsity officials and chain crew.

Locate Dining Facilities for Out-of-Town Games

The week of a game is no time to spend your valuable hours making long distance calls to out-of-town restaurants in an attempt to make meal arrangements for your squad. Follow this plan:

1. Contact the football coach in the town where you will play each road game.
2. Ask for a list of good eating places that he thinks would be large enough to accommodate your squad (plus cheerleaders and other school officials).
3. The out-of-town coach should be able to tell you where other teams usually eat when in town.
4. Be sure to ask the coach to provide phone numbers and names of restaurant managers if available. This alone will save much time.
5. Call each restaurant manager. Tell him what you would like to eat (be specific). Tell him how many people you will bring and approximately how much you plan to spend.
6. Once this information is gathered, record the manager's name, his phone number, and the date of the conversation. Tell him if you decide to eat at his restaurant you will contact him a week prior to the game. The week of the game simply call the restaurant of your choice and place your order.

Secure Dummys on Sleds

Several days before the start of practice have your managers place the dummys on the blocking sleds. Be sure that they are secured tightly and do not "slip." Although they should already have been checked, inspect the dummys for unnoticed tears or cuts. If your budget allows, try to have one or more reserve dummys on hand for use during the season if needed.

Final Check of Transportation for Games

In Chapter 7—July, we suggested that special buses (or other transportation) be ordered. Now that your first game is weeks (or days) away make a list minute call checking:

- How many buses you will need (this might have changed due to early season practice injuries, etc) . . .
- The exact date and time you want the buses to arrive . . .
- Special instructions such as where you will eat after the game, or some special stop that needs to be made along the way . . .
- How the payment will be handled (send a bill? pay at the conclusion of the trip?) . . .

Check Press Box and Field Phones
and Headsets at Stadium

The stadium press box should, by now, be clean and ready for
first game use. Take an assistant coach with you and check the
field-to-press box phones. Insert new batteries if needed in the
phone sets. Check all wiring to be sure it is free from entangle-
ment. Clean the headsets. Make any minor repairs that are necessary. Store the headsets or hang them on hooks along the wall,
ready for the first home game.

Review College Recruiting Rules
with College Prospects

Many high school football players of average ability have stars
in their eyes and see themselves as college heros. It is a good idea
to have a meeting of the entire team early in fall practice to discuss
college recruiting. We try to stress two points to the entire squad.
First, we impress the players with the fact that college football is a
solid step above high school football and takes special dedication
and talent. It isn't for everybody. And second, we want to empha-
size that if we have a player who we feel can play we will do
everything possible to bring that player to the attention of college
recruiters.

The next step is to have a meeting with all senior players who
have shown above-average ability. Be sure to invite the parents of
these players, in fact, you might insist that they attend so that
they, too, can learn about college recruiting. Start by telling the
players that *you* (the coach) cannot "get" a player a scholarship.
You can recommend a player, send films to the colleges, talk to
recruiters, and help fill out information forms. *But in the final
analysis, the college staff must decide if the player is capable of
playing college football and is worthy of financial aid.*

Some college conferences have booklets available on the up-
to-date recruiting regulations such as how many official visits a
prospect can make to a college campus. Warn the players about
accepting "gifts" from coaches or alumni. Encourage them not to
make commitments they do not intend to fulfill. Advise the players

on how to dress when visiting a college campus and how to meet and talk with recruiters.

Be sure to make it clear to the players that a letter of information or a booklet from the football office is *NOT* an offer of scholarship aid. When a football scholarship offer is made it will be in *firm* and *clear* language.

Suggest to your top prospects that they set up a file at home and keep all information sent from college coaches. Record dates of phone calls and what was said. Keep lists of names of recruiters and which colleges they represent. We also tell our players that if they want our help they *must* keep us informed of all meetings, letters, calls, and visits.

Purchase Last Minute Football Items
(Mouthpieces, Helmet Hardware, etc.)

Just as August practice is about to begin make a detailed last-minute check of the small items that perhaps have been overlooked, but will be needed during the season.

Here are a few suggestions:

- mouthpieces
- helmet hardware
- helmet face masks (cages)
- helmet striping or decals
- chin straps
- wrist sweatbands
- practice shorts
- extra kicking tees
- screw driver (for helmet repair)
- ice chest or water cooler
- cleats
- cleat wrench
- shoestrings
- film projector lamp (once your present lamp burns out it might be difficult to find the exact style lamp you need immediately)
- towels (to keep footballs and equipment dry)
- chalk for blackboard
- soap for shower

Discuss Pep Rallies with Principal,
Band, Cheerleaders, etc.

At this point you are probably within a few weeks (or maybe a few days) of your first game. The first pep rally should be planned with great care to make it run smoothly. Although planning pep rallies is probably not your responsibility, you should have some ideas for, and input into, the planning.

The main thing that you as a coach should be concerned with is how the pep rally affects your players. You may prefer a morning pep rally. Maybe the last period of the school day is best for your game day schedule. Let your thoughts be known. By all means, don't let your players be called on to take part in skits, dance, etc. at the pep rally unless that is what you want and believe in. Keep in mind that the band people, the cheerleaders, the principal, or others involved with the planning probably don't understand that the pep rally should be to get the general student body excited about the game. If your players aren't ready to play by game day, I doubt the pep rally will do much good as far as they are concerned. Stress that the rally is to "fire up" the students and give them the same spirit and excitement that the players (hopefully) already have.

Join State Coaching Organization

Most states probably have state coaching organizations which work to better high school athletics. As a professional, each head coach should be a contributing member. Check on the organization in your state and find out what you can do to help the sport that helps you make a living.

Help Plan Touchdown Club Programs

If you are asked, you might want to present some ideas for Touchdown Club weekly programs throughout the season. Many clubs like to see last week's game film. Besides that, there should be a central theme or idea for each program. Let's assume there are ten TD Club meetings (one for each game on your schedule) and that the club meets on Monday night. Here are some program ideas that could encourage attendance and provide variety to the programs:

1. Player's Night—Have your entire squad present. Present each player to the club, giving his position and jersey number. (Players can even wear their jerseys if you prefer).

2. Cheerleader Night—Introduce each girl and the cheerleader sponsor. Let them give a brief report on their activities, their plans for the season, and the work that goes into being a cheerleader.

3. Band Night—Let the band director give TD club members an insight into his program. Certain band members (or the entire band if room permits) should be invited along with majorettes, flag girls, etc.

4. Referee's Night—Invite a top game official to speak to the group. Encourage them to explain any new rules for the season or to give his views on high school football from the official's point of view.

5. Opposing Coach Night—Invite the coach of one of your top opponents, a team you'll play in the next few weeks. Select a coach whom you know well, who has a good relation with your school, and who has a good sense of humor. Be careful not to "put him on the spot" with loaded questions which could cause embarrassment to him or to you.

6. Homecoming Night—Obviously, you will want to use this theme during Homecoming week. It is a good opportunity to inform TD Club members of all Homecoming activities, especially ones in which they can take part. If possible have the Homecoming Queen candidates present. All old grads should be invited to this meeting.

7. Mother's Night—Chances are that most (or all) of the TD Club members are male. At any rate, have a special night where the players' mothers are guests of the club. Introduce each mother along with her son (if present). Be sure to point out in the game films where each "son" is playing.

8. Junior Varsity Night—Invite these players as special guests and provide time for their coaches to make comments on their season. Recognize parents of these players who might be present.

9. All Sports Night—Although the emphasis will still be on football, allow the athletic director to introduce coaches of the

school's other sports (especially the basketball coaches as their season will start soon). Let them give a brief report on their coming
season and perhaps recruit some parents to help with a "booster
club" of their own.

10. Senior Night—For the last meeting of the season put the
spotlight on your seniors and their parents. Introduce each player
and comment on the accomplishments of the seniors during the
past two or three years.

Contact Someone to Operate
P.A. System at Stadium

Hopefully the same person who worked the public address
system for you last fall will do the job again. If you must seek a
new man look for these qualities:

1. A good voice
2. Loyalty to your school and football program
3. Knowledge of the game of football
4. Dependability and promptness
5. Some knowledge of the mechanics of the public address system

Be sure to have a talk with the P.A. announcer prior to the
first game. Remind him that his purpose is to announce starting
lineups and make general announcements to the fans. By no means
is he to pretend he is a "radio announcer" and describe the action
play-by-play (the fans can see it for themselves). Nor is he to
reflect on the judgment of the game officials or in any way offend
the visiting players and fans. A school-related person, such as the
basketball coach, or a male English teacher, may be a good choice
for your P.A. announcer.

Team Photo Day for Press, Fans, etc.

Handing out game uniforms and having 40 to 50 players pose
for pictures is a time-consuming process. You should not have to do
it more than once, because it breaks into your pre-season practice
schedule.

Give plenty of advance notice concerning your "photo day."
Contact newspapers and television stations. Send notes home to
parents and friends of the players. Contact school faculty members

responsible for taking football pictures for the school yearbook and school newspaper. Stress with all of these people that there will be no other picture day and that practice time is too valuable to issue uniforms and take pictures two or three times during the season. Make it clear that all pictures needed for the season should be taken on the day set aside as "team photo day."

Taking photos can be a confusing experience unless the day is well planned. Here are some organizational suggestions:

1. Have your players report one hour before the photographers. Issue uniforms. Have the players dress and remain in the locker room until all are ready.

2. Line the players up in order by jersey numbers starting with the lowest and going to the highest, and take them to the photo area (stadium or practice field).

3. Take all group pictures first (pictures which include all team members, managers, and coaches). Note: pictures taken with players in consecutive order of jersey numbers make identification easier.

4. Make sure that *all* photographers who want group pictures take them while the team is sitting as a group. They won't be this way again.

5. After the group pictures are taken send the players (by jersey number) to the photographers for individual shots. Keep the players in order and as quiet as possible so that directions from the photographer can be heard. After each player has his picture taken he should proceed to the next photographer who needs his picture.

6. After all of the official photographers (from newspaper, TV, school newspaper, etc.) have their pictures the players are free to go with friends and family members for personal photos.

7. Be sure to have several footballs available for all pictures if needed.

See That Stadium Field Is Lined Off for Games

Some coaches have to line their own field during the week (day?) of the game. The schedule will be determined by the location of the game field (near the school or across town), the time available to the coach (does the coach have free time at school?), and the help available (are plenty of managers available? can help be gotten from students in Physical Education classes?).

Other factors to take into consideration before lining the field are these:

● Will your team practice on the game field the day before the game? If so, do you prefer the field to be lined off before or after the practice (it would look nicer after the practice).

● Will some group—the band or drill team—practice on the field the day before the game (flat-soled shoes worn by band members will scatter the line markings if 75-100 band members march across the freshly marked lines).

● What is the weather outlook? Heavy rains for days before the game will mean the field must be marked off perhaps only hours before game time. Forecasts of bad weather might indicate that the field be lined off one or two days in advance.

● Will there be a junior varsity game on the field the day before the varsity game?

If your game field is at a stadium operated by the city government or some recreation department, and whose own personnel are responsible for marking the field, call someone in charge to make sure they are aware of your game.

Final Week-of-Game Checklist

No matter how many plans are made (or how closely this book is followed), there are always anxious moments during the week of the opening game relating to whether every detail of game operation has been taken care of. Mimeograph a checklist similar to this one and review it (whether you play at home or on the road):

_____ Uniforms clean and ready

_____ Game ball ready (have several)

_____ Officials contacted

_____ Ticket takers and security organized

_____ P.A. system and announcer ready

_____ Programs picked up from printer

_____ Program sellers organized

_____ Chains and down markers ready and those who carry them contacted

_____ Game film picked up and photographer ready

_____ Field lined off

_____ Transportation contacted and ready

_____ Statistic charts and statistician ready

_____ Insurance list up to date

_____ Eligibility list up to date

_____ Newspaper, radio and television contacted about the game

_____ Medical kit prepared

_____ Opposing coach contacted by phone concerning game details

_____ Dressing rooms at stadium clean

_____ Pre-game schedule worked out with band, drill team, or pep squad

_____ Cheerleaders contacted

_____ Team doctors contacted

_____ Ambulance (at stadium during the game) contacted

_____ Pre-game or post-game meals ordered

_____ Liquid (or ice) for use during game available

_____ Stadium lights checked

_____ Scoreboard checked

_____ Headset phone (from field to press box) working

_____ Equipment repair kit ready (laces, shoestrings, helmet hardware)

Continue this list to include things unique to your school.

Check Clearance of Eligibility List

Most state high school associations require member schools to file a list of eligible (by grades) players. These sheets should have been returned by now. You must *carefully* check the list against an accurate roster of your players as the roster stands *now*. Some players may have been added at the last minute. Others may have dropped out. Summer school grades (affecting eligibility) of some players may have been late coming in, causing some players not to be on the eligibility list that was sent in.

Have your players answer the roll as you read the names from the eligibility list. If a player enters your first game without being listed on the eligibility roster it could cause a forfeiture of the game.

Call Opposing Coach Concerning Game Accommodations

About a week before an opponent visits your town and school for a game you should contact the head coach. This contact can be made by phone or by letter. Figure 9-1 shows a sample letter, giving particulars about the game and possible accommodations. The same information could be passed along by phone if you prefer.

September 10, 19____

Dear Coach _____,

We are looking forward to our game with your fine team on Friday, September 19th. Game time is 8:00 p.m.

Here is some information concerning your trip to our city. Please let me know if there is any other way we can help.

Directions: You should enter town on highway 44. Come to the second traffic light and turn left. The stadium and the school are three blocks on the right. Follow the "visitors' parking" signs to the back of the stadium. Park your bus next to the visitors' dressing room sign.

Stadium entrance: The visiting players gate is usually open by 5:00 p.m. Mr. John Nelson will meet you and show you the dressing room. If you plan to arrive earlier than 5:00 p.m. let me know so that arrangements can be made.

Dressing room: Your dressing room can accommodate up to 65 players. Shower facilities and two water fountains are available. Mr. Nelson will provide you with a key to the dressing room which you can return after the game.

Warm-up area: When you take the field for warm-ups please use the south end of the field near the scoreboard. Your team will be seated on the west side of the field across from the press box.

Starting lineup: Please have two written starting lineups available thirty minutes before the game. One will be for our P.A. announcer and the other for use by our radio station.

Pre-game: Our band will take the field at about 7:45 p.m. (or as soon as you have completed your warm-ups) for a brief pre-game show. The National Anthem will be at 7:55 p.m.

Phones: Headsets and press box phones are available. Please check these out at least 30 minutes before gametime and let me know if there are any problems.

Officials: Our officials are from the ——————— Association headed by Mr. ——————.

Half-time drinks: We will provide enough soft drinks for your players, managers, coaches, and cheerleaders. Please locate these *before* the game and let me know if you have enough. The drinks will be iced and in the cooler in the rear of your dressing room. Cheerleaders can pick up their drinks at the concession stand on the north side of the stadium.

Doctors: Our two team doctors, Dr. Kelley and Dr. Richardson, will be at the game and will be either on our sidelines or seated directly behind our bench. Let us know if you need medical help.

Hospital-Ambulance: An ambulance will be at the game and will be located near the south gate, under the scoreboard. Our hospital is approximately five minutes from the stadium. Leave the north end of the stadium heading west on Lee

Drive. The hospital can be seen as you approach the fourth traffic light.

News Media: Mr. Dix from our local newspaper has indicated that he would like to talk with you after the game at your convenience.

Meals: Here is a list of places where other teams have eaten while in town.

(List name of each restaurant, the owner or manager's name, and the phone number.)

Let us know if there is any other way we can help.

Sincerely,

_____ (your name)

Figure 9-1

Order Pre-game and/or Out-of-Town Meals

In Chapter 8—August it was suggested that dining facilities for out-of-town games be located. Several days before making an out-of-town trip contact the restaurant of your choice and place your order. Most restaurant owners are eager for your business and will offer reduced rates. You should demand reasonable rates because you are bringing him hundreds of dollars of business.

Be sure that you and the restaurant owner agree on exactly what you are ordering (for example, are you getting ½ or ¼ of a fried chicken . . . baked potatoes or french fries?). This can save time and confusion later. Also, be sure the drinks and dessert (if any) are included in the price. Determine if tips to waitresses will be necessary. Ask the owner if fans of your team will be welcome after the game (some restaurants stay open *only* for the team and do not wish extra short-order business). Give the owner an approximate time of your arrival (cheerleaders may arrive earlier than the team).

Before leaving for the game be sure to write down the phone number of the restaurant and the owner's name in case you are delayed and need to call.

Mail Tickets and Complimentary Passes to Opponents

One week before your first home game, mail tickets and complimentary passes to the head coach or athletic director of the school you are playing. If you have played the team before, you should have a good idea of the number of tickets to send. Here are some things to help you determine the number to send:

1. What was the size of the crowd last season when you played?
2. Is the opponent from a town close by (they will bring more fans) or from far away (few fans)?
3. How important is the game (your arch rival or a team that stirs little excitement)?
4. Is a championship or play-off berth at stake?
5. Is the weather likely to affect the crowd (late in the season the weather may have turned very cold)?
6. Does your opponent have the tradition of bringing a large following?

Complimentary passes should be discussed weeks prior to the game. You may wish to send from one to fifty or more (or none at all). This will depend on the relations between schools. However, it is a good idea to have in writing the number of tickets sent, so that the following season you will *receive* the same number that you sent this season.

Final Concession Stand Check

The concession stand may be operated by your team parents, the band, the pep squad, the Booster Club, or the school clubs. You may have nothing to do with concessions. As a coach, you should not have this worry. However, for those of you who do here is a last-minute checklist:

- Plenty of workers who know what time to arrive
- Keys given to the proper people
- Ice
- Cups
- Coffee maker

- Soft drinks
- Crackers and chips
- Candy
- Popcorn machine, popcorn, butter, salt, bags
- Hotdogs, hamburgers, sandwiches, buns, mustard, catsup, etc.
- Peanuts

Visit the concession stand several days before the game to be sure it is swept out and clean. Check the light switch and the power outlets to be sure they work.

Pick Up Game Programs and Distribute to Program Sellers

Due to late-arriving rosters most programs will not be available until several days before the first game. Arrange to have them picked up and delivered to the people in charge of selling the programs. Perhaps a parent or member of the Booster Club could handle this chore for you. When the programs are picked up at the printing office have someone make a final proofreading of the material. If a glaring error has been made, there may be time to correct it.

Post-Game Laundry Delivery and Pick-Up

After each game (home or away) the uniforms should be taken to the laundry as soon as possible. Plan ahead who is to sack the uniforms and who is to deliver them to the laundry. Call the laundry and let them know several days ahead that your uniforms will be brought in "on Saturday morning about 10:00 o'clock" so that they can start work on them immediately.

Be sure to tell the people at the laundry exactly when you need the uniforms back (you may play a Thursday or a Saturday game instead of a Friday game) and who will pick them up. Give an accurate acount of the number of uniforms to the laundry so that there will be no misunderstanding as to the number to be returned (this will change from week to week as injured players do and don't dress out).

By all means, don't forget to pick the uniforms up a day or two before you need them. Don't wait until the day of the game and risk having the laundry close early.

Report Game Scores and Highlights

Select one person, such as your statistician, who attends all your games (both home and road) and who has a good knowledge of football, and ask this person to be responsible for calling in your scores and highlights after each game. This person has a very important job and can be responsible for a "good writeup" in the newspaper and good coverage on the radio and television stations.

Before your first game sit down with this person and make a small list of every newspaper, radio, and TV station in your area. Include the telephone number and the name of a reporter or announcer from that particular news medium. Ask your "game reporter" to keep this list with him and to telephone your scores and highlights immediately after each game.

Tell your *reporter* to follow these suggestions:

1. State your school and name and purpose. Say, for example, "I wish to report a high school football score for the Central High of Macon vs. _____ High game played tonight. My name is _____."

2. Speak clearly. Know what you plan to say before you call.

3. Have all stats written out before you so time will not be wasted in adding numbers, etc.

4. Give your report in a simple, clear manner. Talk slowly and spell all names so that there can be no misunderstanding. Here is an example of a brief game report . . .

Central High of Macon defeated _____ High of _____ (city) in Macon tonight by the score of 14-0. The win makes Central's record 3-0 while _____ High drops to 2-1. Scoring for Central was Shannon Hall (S-h-a-n-n-o-n H-a-l-l) who had a 9 yd. run in the first Qt. and Todd Jackson (T-o-d-d J-a-c-k-s-o-n) who returned a punt 54 yds. in the third Qt. Both extra points were kicked by Lee Stevens (L-e-e S-t-e-v-e-n-s). Leading rusher for Central was Hall with 122 yds. on 16 carries. Tommy Wilder (T-o-m-m-y W-i-l-d-e-r) had two interceptions for Central. Game stats:

	Central	_____ High
First Downs	15	8
Yd. Rushing	211	143
Yd. Passing	101	72
Att/Comp/Int.	9/6/0	10/5/2
Punting	36.1	34.9
Fumbles lost	1	0

After giving the general information and stats ask if the writer/announcer wants additional information. Be prepared to give him what he wants . . . leading tackler . . . opponent's scoring . . . number of penalties, etc.

It would be a good idea to contact all news media in the area before the first game and give them the name of your reporter. Tell them to "expect his call every Friday night for the next ten weeks."

Weekly Team Publicity

Football teams receive varying degrees of publicity depending on the size of the town, the size of the school, other teams in the area, and the school's won/lost record. You can help your team's publicity by providing "inside" information to reporters. This can be done in two ways, by phone and by mail. Of course, phone is quicker and must be used at times. However, to be fair to all media personnel you will need to mimeograph (or make carbon copies of) your material, sending it equally to all newspapers, radio, and TV stations. Keep the media informed and up to date on:

- Individual statistics
- Team statistics
- Injuries, especially those that may cause a player to be held out of a game
- Records that have been set, or are close to being set
- Key position changes among players
- Changes in starting line-up
- Human interest stories about players, managers, or coaches
- Travel plans to out of town games
- Opponent's key players and team records
- Touchdown Club meeting dates
- Weekly award winners (if you give weekly awards)

Remember, the key to good relations with the media is to treat them all fairly. Avoid giving one reporter advance notice of developing stories.

Contact Opponents About Trading Films

Hopefully you will be able to film all or some of your games this season. If you do film, you will have to make a decision on whether to trade films with a future opponent. If no trading is to take place, you must do a better job of scouting each time your future opponent plays.

Now, before the season starts, you should contact the coaches of teams on your schedule and decide if one or more game films are to be traded. Keeping up with these films during the tight fall schedule will take some planning. Use a chart like the one in Figure 9-2 to keep up with where your films are. Assign an assistant to handle the trading of films, but have him keep you informed each time one of your films is sent out.

FILM LOCATION CHART

Film: Central High vs. _____

Sent to: _____High School

    Address _____

    City, State _____

    Coach _____

Date sent: _____19____

Film delivered by: _____ mail

                              _____ bus

                              _____ person-to-person contact

                              _____ other (explain)

Terms: _____ Send in exchange for ____ (number) reels of opponent's film

              _____ No exchange of films from opponent

              _____ Postage or bus transportation cost to be paid by sender

              _____ Postage or bus transportation cost to be paid by receiver

Date film is to be returned: _____19____

Film to be returned by: _____ mail

                              _____ bus

                              _____ person-to-person contact

                              _____ other (explain)

Check here when film(s) has been returned and all obligations are cleared: _____

Signature of coach handling film transaction: _____

Figure 9-2

Complimentary Passes Before First Home Game

Every coach has a number of people who have contributed in some personal way to the welfare of his team. It is a nice gesture to reward these people with one or several complimentary passes to your first home game. The number of passes you hand out will depend on the number of people who have really helped you, the gate receipts you expect from your first game, and the present financial situation of your athletic budget.

Be sure that the passes you distribute are handed out in plenty of time to prevent the recipient from purchasing advance tickets to the game. Here are some ideas concerning who might be on your complimentary pass list:

- Team doctor
- School administrators and faculty members
- Maintenance workers who help with field and stadium upkeep
- Booster Club leaders
- Statistician
- Former school coaches and administrators still living in the area
- City government leaders (mayor, city councilmen)
- Policemen
- Parents of senior players
- Anyone who helps team with transportation or meals

Make First Contact with Possible Football Banquet Speaker

Whether your team has its football banquet in November, December, or January it is not too early to line up a good speaker for the occasion. First, you must decide the type of speaker you want. Do you want a local person or someone from out of town? Do you want a college coach, a high school coach, or someone who is not a coach (such as a college or professional player)? Are you looking for a big-name personality, or for a lesser-known person who is a proven speaker? Are you looking for a speaker who will draw a crowd and make the banquet a financial success, or for someone noted for quieter, more inspirational talks to the players? Do you want someone to humor and entertain the crowd?

After deciding on the *type* of speaker you want make a list of those people who best fit your needs and rate them first choice, second choice, etc. Talk with others involved in the banquet preparations about the financial aspects of getting a speaker. How much money is available for the speaker's transportation? Will he need to stay overnight? Does he charge a fee for speaking, and if so, how much? Once these matters have been decided write him a letter like the one that follows, making the initial inquiry as to his availability.

September ——, 19——

Dear ——————————,

The Central High of Macon football team is planning its annual football banquet and would be very pleased and honored to have you as our guest speaker.

The banquet will be held in early December several weeks after the close of the regular season. The dates we have in mind are Monday night, December 2nd, Thursday night, December 5th, or Monday night, December the 9th. Please let us know at your earliest convenience if you will be able to come, and if so, which of the three dates best suits your schedule.

Our Touchdown Club will provide travel expenses as well as motel expenses if you wish to stay overnight. A speaker's fee of $150 is also available.

We are looking forward to hearing from you and hope you can be with us. If you can come, I will be in touch with you several weeks in advance of the banquet to finalize the details of your visit.

Sincerely,

————————————

Keep Accurate List of Film Departures and Returns

This is an end-of-the-month reminder to continue to keep up with your game films and who has each one. The chart on page 143 can be beneficial in keeping up with your films. If any school or coach is late in returning a film, call him immediately. Failure to have one of your films might prevent you from being able to trade off with another school, which could cost you an opportunity to "scout by film" a future opponent.

Speaking Engagement Schedule

Now that the season is beginning you, as the football coach of your school, will be asked to address many groups. Some of the groups will be more "formal" than others. For example, you might be asked to talk to local civic clubs with several hundred businessmen in attendance. Or you may speak each week to your Touchdown or Booster Club as it meets to view the game film of the past week. You will need to speak at times to your school student body.

Keep a speaking engagement schedule on your office desk. Check it carefully each day and know several days in advance of each speaking engagement.

Start a file dealing with speaking material. Each time you see a story, joke, poem, or illustration that could be worked into one of your speeches drop it into the file for later use.

As you plan your speech, be sure you relate it to the age of your listeners, and to their particular interests. If you speak to the same type of group (such as Booster Club) each week, be careful not to repeat your material. After making a speech, file and date your notes.

Plan Post-season Football Banquet with
Touchdown Club and School Officials

Hopefully, you have a Touchdown Club (or Booster Club) that will take some responsibility for holding a banquet for your varsity football players at the end of the season. Of course, the school will be involved with the planning and possibly the financial end of the banquet, too. If the banquet is to be held in December, January, or February it is certainly not too early to make definite banquet plans. Here are some items that will need planning:

1. Banquet Date—Check your school calendar to avoid any conflict with school-related activities such as basketball games, P.T.A. programs, etc. Also check your town's social schedule to avoid holidays, civic events, plays, etc.
2. Decorations Committee—Develop a "theme" for the banquet. Place responsible people on this important committee.
3. Banquet Location—Decide where the banquet will be held and reserve the room (be sure the place is large enough for the anticipated crowd).
4. Speaker—see Chapter 9.

After these four items have been decided upon, the banquet is well underway and only the final details need to be arranged.

Refer to Chapter 1—January for a final checklist of things to do as time for the banquet gets nearer.

Mid-season Review of Offense and Defense

If you are winning, and hopefully you are, this recommendation will not apply to you. If you are losing, the reason may not be traced directly to your offensive and defensive styles, but rather to a lack of talented players. However, all teams need to take a look at themselves at mid-season and re-evaluate what they are doing. For example:

. . is your best running back carrying the football enough?

. . are you taking advantage of motion by your offensive backs as you hoped you could?

. . has some new pass receiver shown his ability which will enable you to pass the ball more?

. . does your trapping game need more work?

. . do you need to do more double-team blocking due to the size of your linemen?

. . has your goal line defense held up in game situations?

. . are any players playing "out of position"?

. . are you having communication problems between the sidelines and your signal caller?

. . should you stunt and blitz more (or less) when on defense?

. . now that some new players have experience can we two-platoon rather than play the same people both ways?

Check In and Clean Any Equipment
Not Being Used

By this time in the season you have probably had several players leave the squad. Some have left due to injury which will prevent them from playing again this season. Others, especially on the junior high level, may have dropped from the squad for a variety of reasons.

Do not leave their equipment lying around in the locker room. Each player must always be made to turn in his own equipment. (This must be made clear when you issue equipment at the beginning of the season.) Check in each piece of equipment and charge the player for any equipment not returned. Require the player to turn in his equipment *clean* just as it was given to him. The shoes should be polished and the laces tied together. The jersey should be washed and folded. Pads should be taken out of the pants.

Should equipment be turned in unclean for some reason, have it cleaned immediately. You may need to reissue it to another player as replacement equipment at any time.

Mid-season Player Equipment Check

Some players probably are using the same equipment that was issued to them last spring, or perhaps last fall (and was stored in duffle bags during the off-season to avoid having to reissue). It is a responsibility of the coach to take a mid-season equipment check to see if the equipment of each player is still safe. Look for these things:

• *Helmet* . . . look for small cracks around the edge. Be sure no hardware (screws, etc.) is missing, and that the facemask is firmly attached. Have the player put the helmet on and be sure it isn't too small or too large.

• *Shoulder pads* . . . check all straps and buckles. Replace laces that are wearing thin. Look for cracks in the shoulder padding.

• *Hip pads, thigh pads, knee pads* . . . be sure the padding is firm and without tears.

• *Jersey* . . . the main concern here is whether the jersey is offering protection for the player from the weather. A thinner jersey was probably issued in August, but the player may now need a much heavier material in his jersey.

• *Pants* . . . exchange, or repair immediately, any pants with small rips or tears.

• *Shoes* . . . this is one of the critical areas of a player's equipment. Be sure the pair he is wearing still fits. Check for cleats wearing through the soles. Replace thin or broken shoestrings.

Select Post-Season Awards and Secure Bids

Now that the season is well underway you can give some thought to what post-season awards you plan to give at the football banquet. Look at your financial situation and determine the amount you plan to spend for trophies, plaques, etc. Talk with your other coaches and decide which trophy categories are most important to give. Choose from a list such as this:

- Most Valuable Player
- Most Valuable Offensive Player
- Most Valuable Defensive Player
- Most Valuable Offensive Lineman
- Most Valuable Receiver
- Most Valuable Offensive Back
- Most Valuable Defensive Lineman
- Most Valuable Linebacker
- Most Valuable Defensive Back
- Most Valuable Special Teams Player (kicking game)
- Best Hustler
- Best Spirit
- Most Improved Defensive Player
- Most Improved Offensive Player
- Offensive Rookie Of The Year
- Defensive Rookie Of The Year
- Best Scholastic Average
- Coaches' Trophy (for an all-round good player and person)
- Senior (junior, sophomore) of the Year
- Leading Tackler
- Leading Rusher
- Leading Passer
- Most Interceptions
- Most Fumble Recoveries
- Leading Receiver (most catches)

After you have determined the number of awards you plan to give, contact several sporting goods dealers and/or trophy shops. Let them give bid prices on the total amount of your awards. Remember that there is a great markup of trophies and plaques so demand a good discount. After you have selected the company that you will deal with, go pick out the awards you want and have the company prepare the lettering on the awards. After the season is over, they can add the name of the person who receives the award.

Some schools like to have several businesses around town sponsor a trophy. It gives the business a little publicity and is no great financial burden to anyone. For example, your local radio station may give the Most Valuable Lineman trophy. Announce at the banquet later in the year who sponsors each award. *However*, be sure that the selection of the award winner remains in *your* hands. Never let an outside business name the winner.

Call This Month's Opponents

In Chapter 9—September, it was suggested that you call your opponents to discuss game time, meals, directions, etc. Be sure to do the same for this month's opponents.

Meals Check

As each new week approaches you need to make last minute checks with restaurants concerning:

- pre-game meals for your team
- post-game meals for your team
- meal arrangements for visiting teams
- financial arrangements

Transportation Check

Contact personally the person in charge of your travel arrangements for this month. Review the time that you wish the transportation to be at your school ready to travel. Review financial arrangements. Discuss any problems that you might have had last month as your team traveled to out-of-town games.

Film Check

Talk with your game film photographer. Discuss items such as:

- The quality of films you are getting
- Changes in lighting, etc. that may be needed
- Changes in game coverage that you may want (a wider angle picture of your kick-off team when it covers the kick-off, or more shots of the scoreboard to check down and distance between plays)
- Film delivery (is it satisfactory?)
- How much film is available for the rest of the season?

Laundry Check

By mid-season you may need to make changes in your laundry arrangements. For example, you may have been taking Friday night's game uniforms to the laundry on Saturday morning only to find out that the laundry doesn't wash the uniforms until Monday. Taking the uniforms on Monday may suit your schedule better than taking them on Saturday.

Also, offer any suggestions to the laundry concerning your uniforms. Don't be afraid to change laundries if you are not satisfied with the service you are getting. By all means, be sure you are getting prompt service. You certainly should not have to worry about whether your uniforms will be ready by the next game.

Speaking Engagement Schedule

By this time of the year you may find yourself speaking to so many groups that some of the same people are hearing you every week or so (this is especially true with people attending Booster Club meetings). Try to keep from repeating your stories. Taking notes of each "speech" you make can help eliminate this.

Even though your time is limited now, be sure to spend some time preparing what you plan to say to a group. If they take time to come and listen to you, they deserve some new and fresh points of view concerning your football team that they can't get anywhere else but from you.

Secure Films of Future Opponents

Try to call at the beginning of each month and line up the films that you will need to "scout" this month's opponents. By this time of the season you may have seen some of the teams play personally and feel you do not need a film. Remember, that to get a film you generally have to give a film. Is what you are *getting* worth what you must *give up* to get it? Some opponents may have poor quality films (bad lighting, poor camera work). Trade only with those teams whose films match yours in quality.

Check Junior Varsity Personnel with JV Coaches

By now it should be mid-season of your junior varsity schedule. Those players have had an opportunity to get organized and play several games. Arrange a meeting with your JV coaches and discuss these things:

1. How many players are on the team? Are there enough quarterbacks, snappers, etc. to field a representative team?
2. Have any players had serious injuries that you should know about?
3. Who are the best offensive and defensive people?
4. Is enough safe equipment available?
5. Do the JV coaches need help with taping injuries?
6. Are enough footballs, kicking tees, and medical supplies available to suit their needs for the rest of the season?
7. Do the JV coaches need any help from the varsity coaches in teaching fundamentals (such as trapping, or punt coverage)?

When talking to the JV coaches be sure to take a long, hard look at which team (JV or varsity) each player is on. Several JV players may be playing well enough to be brought up to the varsity. Injuries to key varsity players might also be a reason to move several JV players up. Perhaps you have some varsity players who aren't seeing much action and would benefit by playing the last few games with the JV squad. Before moving a player up or down between JV and varsity call him in and explain the reason for the move. A younger JV player might need to be asked if he feels ready to move up. An older varsity player needs to be told how playing several JV games will make him a better player.

Mid-Season Publicity and Stats to Media

Your local radio, TV, and newspaper reporters probably have *some* statistics concerning your season. But by mid-season their records probably need updating. Have your statistician compile your mid-season stats and mimeograph them, sending copies to all media people in the area.

Include all the usual stats such as rushing yardage for each running back, pass completions and yardage for your quarterbacks, and kicking averages. But also include some stats which they might not be aware of. For example:

- Of the five games you have played, three have been against teams rated in the Top Ten in the state.
- Your team has not lost a home game since losing the home opener a year ago.
- The team has not allowed a TD pass to be thrown against them this season.
- If your top running back keeps up his present *yards gained per carry average* he will set a new school record.
- No one has returned a punt or kick-off for a touchdown against our team in two and a half years.
- The team tied a school record by intercepting five passes in one game. This occurred against _____ High School the second game of this season.

Call This Month's Opponents

Whether you are having a winning or losing season you must continue to do the little things that will mark you and your team as *first class*. If your season is not going well in the won-loss column it is sometimes difficult to place a telephone call to an opponent and talk about the details of your up-coming game, But it must be done.

Review these things with a team visiting in your town:

- Directions to the stadium
- Location of dressing rooms
- Bus parking facilities
- Time schedule of events surrounding the game (band, etc.)
- What color jersey to wear
- Possible eating establishments for the visiting team and/or fans
- Game officials

When talking to the opposing coach you might remember to discuss items of future interest such as:

- Return of films that have been borrowed
- Possible date for scheduling a game for next fall
- Possible changes in officials for next fall's game

Meal Check

Contact out-of-town restaurants and finalize plans for eating before and/or after your final games of the season. If you have already made contact with the restaurant owner early in the fall, call him again with the *exact* number in your party, and the exact items you desire on your menu. You might also double-check on prices since they might have increased since earlier in the fall when you made first contact.

Transportation Check

By this time you have a good indication as to whether your transportation is reliable or not. Nothing can be more irritating to a coach and his team than transportation that arrives late for an out-of-town trip or even a trip to your own stadium. If you have had problems with this, either call the manager of the transportation company and be assured of better service, or make other travel arrangements. *A reminder to the coach:* When making an out-of-town trip *always* have a map available showing the best route to the city where you are playing and also a map showing directions from the city limits to the stadium! Getting lost and wandering about looking for a stadium in a strange city plays on the nerves of players and coaches alike.

Laundry Check

Continue to work closely with your laundry to insure having game uniforms ready for pick-up several days before each game. Now that the season is drawing to a close make some mental notes (for use next fall) concerning the type of service your laundry rendered your team.

- Was the service prompt?
- Were uniforms always cleaned properly (especially *white* jerseys and pants)
- Were any items ever lost?
- Were the prices fair and competitive with other laundries in the area? (You might need to check prices with other laundries before next fall.)

- Did the laundry provide pick-up and delivery service or did you have to handle this yourself?

Film Return Check

Talk with your assistant who handles the sending and receiving of game films. Ask him to provide you with a list of films that have not been returned along with the names of coaches who have these films.

Send a note, or better still, call the coaches who have not returned your films. Demand that they be returned at once. Here are several good reasons why you need your films in hand at the close of the regular season:

- When a coach does not return your film immediately after use there is a tendency to place your film on a shelf and forget it is there. The coach later may not even realize he has your film.
- If your team is in a play-off, you may need the film for trading purposes.
- College coaches want to begin seeing film on your college prospects.
- The films may be needed for showing to Touchdown Club members or to civic groups.

Scout Possible Play-off Opponents

Scouting a team that you will meet in a play-off game is quite different from regular season scouting. Since *regular* season schedules are made up anywhere from six months to two years (or longer) in advance, you have plenty of time to compile a scouting report on your regular season opponents. You can spend the summer looking at last season's films of them. There is leisure time to talk with other coaches concerning their strengths and weaknesses. You can plan every move you want to make in detail. But when meeting a *play-off* opponent you will probably have *one week or less* to make preparations. Here are things to do when you are suddenly faced with limited time in which to prepare for a playoff opponent:

1. Call every coach who has played your play-off opponent this season. Some will provide you with valuable information.

Others won't. Call the more experienced coaches first. You often will have to rely on their judgments and evaluations. The main general questions to ask are . . . what offensive sets do they use . . . which set is their favorite . . . what basic plays do they use . . . do they throw dropback, play-action, or sprint-out type passes . . . what basic defense do they employ . . . do they stunt often . . . if so, how . . . describe their goal line defense . . . how good is their kicking game (returns, extra points, punts, etc.) . . . who are their best players, and their weakest . . . what is the general philosophy of the head coach (is he a "defensive" coach . . . does he like to throw . . . is he noted for having a weak kicking game).

2. *Travel* to get films of your play-off opponent. There is no time to send films through the mail. The films will confirm the information given by the coaches in the previous (#1) statements. You may need to send several assistants traveling in different directions to get these films from around the state.

3. Call special weekend staff meetings. You may need to meet all day on Saturday (after you have played on a Friday night and after you have learned the identity of your play-off opponent). You and your staff must compile a whole season's information on your play-off opponent in just a matter of hours.

4. Call a team meeting on Saturday (if you played on Friday night). You may always have had a team meeting on Saturday morning, but during the play-off season it can be vital. They must, just as you and your staff members, absorb a great amount of information quickly and the sooner they get started, the more they will learn.

5. Make quick changes in your bulletin board information. As you pick up films of your opponent from coaches who have played them try also to get a copy of the game program which will contain individual photos of the players you will meet this weekend. Post them on the bulletin board along with all the other information you have gathered.

6. Look back over newspaper sports pages that you can locate (perhaps you have saved some—or make a trip to the library and look over their stacks). Find write-ups of your play-off opponent's regular season games. By reading the write-ups you can often determine if they are good at making second half comebacks, or how many yards they usually are penalized each game. Little facts like this can help shape your game plan or give clues as to how they might play against you.

Just remember that *any* team you meet in the play-offs has plenty of good qualities or else they wouldn't be playing. Do not take any team lightly regardless of how they might look on film or what reports you get from other coaches.

Clean Out Press Box, Store Amplifier, Headsets, etc.

Now that you've played your last game and the season is over, you must start a whole new process of activities. A few short months ago you were leading *into* the season. Now you must *close down* many of these activities, and this takes an equal amount of planning and organization. One of the first steps is to "winterize" your stadium—that is, to secure it until next fall. Start with the press box. Sweep it, dust it, pick up all trash, and straighten the chairs and tables. Cut off any sources of electricity (if desired). Make any minor repairs that are needed.

Take the amplifier used for the public address system and store it in a safe place (perhaps in the school vault). Secure any loose wires. Cover anything that is to be left to prevent dust from gathering inside.

Collect the headsets used in field-to-press box communication. Store these in a safe place, or if they are to be left in the press box, be sure they are protected from dampness and dust.

Leave the press box in good shape to begin the next season. It will save time and work next fall if all you have to do is "open the doors, dust, and begin operation."

Take Up Senior Equipment

As your season draws to a close, begin announcing the day and date that equipment will be taken up. Post the date on your locker room bulletin board. Announce it over and over again at practice. Stress that *all* players turn in equipment on *that* day, so that equipment will not straggle in over the next few weeks.

Seniors will be handing in their equipment for the last time. Do not accept any equipment that has not been cleaned. Shoes should be polished and laces tied together. Place the shoe size on a small piece of tape and stick it to the back heel of the shoes in case someone else will need them next fall. Make each senior clean his helmet, fold his practice pants, and leave his pads inside the girdle (for girdle hip pads). And, most important of all, be sure the practice jersey is turned in. These items are coveted by all players, but will cost you a good deal of money if they are not turned in.

Check and Store Returning Players' Equipment

There are several ways to handle equipment of players who will return to play for you next fall.

1. You can take up all equipment just as you did with your seniors. However, when spring or fall practice starts you will have to go through the long process of reissuing each piece of equipment to every player.

2. You can have returning players leave their equipment in their lockers. This idea isn't bad providing: (a) the locker room isn't *open* so that outsiders can bother the equipment, and (b) the equipment is left clean and organized in the locker.

3. The way we prefer is to issue each returning player an equipment travel bag. If your school doesn't have these, ask each player to bring a duffle bag from home. Have each player come in on the designated equipment take-up day. Ask each player to gather his equipment and report to the equipment room. With several assistant coaches helping, quickly check each item of equipment. Be sure that it is clean. Then ask the player if he wishes to exchange any of his equipment. One player might have a pair of pants that need repair. Take these up and issue him a new pair. Another player might want a larger pair of shoulder pads. Make this exchange. (Many players will need no exchanges at all.) Once a returning player is satisfied with his equipment he will place it in his travel (duffle) bag. Label the bag with the player's name (use tape applied to the bag). Then stack the equipment bags in a safe, dry place. When spring (or fall) practice starts simply give each player his travel bag and he is ready to go. You will not have to take time to issue anything. This process of bagging up returning players' equipment, if well organized, should not take over an hour for a squad of 40-50 players.

Note: Obviously, some new equipment will be ordered and will arrive before next fall's practice starts. When you begin fall practice you may have to take up some old pants, or shoes, and issue the new ones. But at least each player will not have to be fitted and sized with *every* thing he needs.

Store Game Equipment

1. Be sure all game jerseys and game pants have been collected from the players, or picked up from the laundry.
2. Check to be sure each item is cleaned and folded.
3. Count each item and record for your inventory records.
4. Make notes of repairs or replacements that will be needed.
5. Place the jerseys and pants in trunks or heavy cardboard boxes.
6. Place the trunks or boxes in a dry place.
7. Secure the trunks with locks, or the boxes with tape.
8. Store the equipment in a room that can be locked.

Make Note of Game Equipment
Needed Before Next Season

Once all game equipment has been collected for storage do these things:

- Count each item of game equipment.
- Discard any piece of equipment that cannot be used and subtract from your equipment count.
- Separate any items of equipment that need repairs.
- Estimate the size of your team for next fall.
- Compare your game equipment on hand with your estimated needs for the fall.
- Make a written account of your needs. Be careful to record the *sizes* of pants that must be replaced and the *numbers* needed on replacement jerseys.

Select Award Winners (for Banquet)

Selecting a *few* members of a football team to receive awards while the rest of the players receive nothing is always a problem. Before we look at methods to select award winners consider this idea. Go ahead and give a *limited* number of trophies and plaques to those few individuals who are *really* outstanding. By a limited number we mean about four or less awards. Then take the *extra* award money in your budget and purchase small inexpensive "awards" for *every* team member. These awards could be:

- A team picture (maybe the Booster Club could add frames).
- A certificate certifying that the player was a member of the varsity football team in 19_____. The certificate could be signed by the head coach, the athletic director and the principal (frames could be used here too).
- A small medal. These are relatively inexpensive and could feature a football player on the front and the year or the team won-loss record stamped on the back.

This idea—giving each team member some small something—often eases the hurt of those players who don't receive any of the major awards.

When selecting your major award winners there are four paths you can take. Each has advantages and disadvantages. Decide which is best in your particular situation:

1. Let the organization that buys the trophy (or plaque) choose the winner. Some schools allow the local radio station or newspaper, or a local sporting goods dealer to provide a certain trophy, such as the lineman of the year award.

Advantage: The coach is not burdened with making the decision.

Disadvantage: The people choosing the winner are not really that knowledgeable about the working of your team and will generally tend to select a "name" player rather than one who really does the work. Politics can get involved.

2. Let the coaches pick the winners.

Advantage: You—the coach—really knows who should win the award. You have seen the players at practice as well as in the games and you alone know if the player is doing what you have asked him to do.

Disadvantage: Some disappointed players and parents (especially parents!) will usually criticize your choices.

3. Let the players pick the winners. Hand out ballots to each varsity player and let them vote secretly. This should be done near the last week of the season. Do it without warning so that players will not have time to get together and talk over who they plan to vote for.

Advantage: Players know pretty well who does the job and who doesn't. No player or parent can complain about who wins the awards since the winners are selected by their peers.

Disadvantage: No real disadvantage. This is really a good system to use. However, the head coach should count the ballots and make adjustments in case:

(a) It is obvious that some deserving player has been left out due to a voting misunderstanding. For example, you might want your split ends to be counted as offensive linemen in the Lineman of the Year vote, yet some of your players might not recognize this and leave an outstanding player off their ballots.

(b) It is obvious that a top player is not receiving votes due to his lack of popularity in the proper "social" circles.

4. Let statistics determine the winners: An excellent way to select your award winners. State at the beginning of the season that trophies will be given to the players who:

- Lead in rushing yardage
- Catch the most passes
- Make the most tackles
- Recover the most fumbles
- Etc. . . .

Advantage: Players know well in advance what they have to do to win an award at the banquet. If they don't win, it is their own fault.

Disadvantage: Some awards that you might want to give such as *Most Spirited Player* or *Best Hustler* cannot be measured in statistics.

Select Jacket and Letter Winners

As the season ends you must make a decision on who are to be awarded football letters (and jackets or sweaters if this is your school policy). This decision is not easy. Some coaches have tried to establish a firm guideline such as "anyone who plays in sixteen quarters will be awarded a letter." This might be O.K. except for two things: one, who has time to keep up with exactly how many quarters forty or fifty players see action in. And, two, what happens if a key team member plays in the first three and one-half games (14 quarters), scores five touchdowns, intercepts two passes, leads the team in tackles . . . then breaks a leg and is out for the season. Shouldn't this player get a letter? By the sixteen quarter rule he can't.

Awarding letters should be left to the discretion of the head coach (with advice from the assistants). With a squad of 40 players, you might have no trouble deciding whether to letter the top 20-25 players. Of course, they deserve to win letters. And you might not have trouble with the last 5 players. They probably don't deserve a letter. Your trouble will come with those 10 to 15 players who saw *some* action, but not a lot. These are the people whom you spotted in and out of the game. Some might even have helped you win, in some small way.

If you fail to give a marginal player a letter, he might become discouraged to the point of losing confidence in himself, especially if a player just barely above him in ability did receive a letter.

If you *do* give a letter to a marginal player, he might feel that he has done all there is to do and has "reached his goal." Of course, this is not correct, but the feeling might be there just the same. In fact, once the player has his letter (and jacket or sweater) he may choose not to play next fall.

There is no easy answer to awarding letters. Just decide on a policy that you believe in and that you can live with, and then stick to it.

Compile Statistics

Sit down with your statistician and compile a complete list of seasonal statistics. Use your game films to back up your statistics or to correct errors. For example, your statistician may list a certain punt as 46 yards long, but others insist it went further. A check of the game film will confirm the punt went 56 and not 46 yards.

Once the statistics are compiled mimeograph copies and distribute to players, coaches, school officials, and Booster Club people as well as to all the news media.

Use the seasonal statistic sheets (see Figure 6-3) that were used for each individual game to compile your stats. Often a newspaper reporter may keep some statistic that is not on your statistic sheet. *If the statistic can be confirmed to your satisfaction*, use it in your final stat sheet.

Season Review with News Media

Reporters from your local newspaper and radio stations are probably interested in doing a final analysis of your season. They need your help.

1. Arrange individual meetings with reporters, or perhaps invite all of them at once to meet with you to wrap up the season. The meeting could be in your office. If funds are available, it would be nice to meet at a local restaurant, with your athletic department picking up the bill.

2. Start the meeting by giving out final statistic sheets. Go over the stats pointing out those that especially influenced your season. For example, you might note that your extra point kicker made 20 of 21 kicks and that you won three games by one point.

3. Discuss the highlights of each game, who did the scoring, who made the great defensive plays, etc.

4. Reflect on the turning points in your season. Example: You might point out that you had considered the first two games of the season your toughest. But after winning the first 13-7 on a 4th quarter punt return, and winning the second 9-7 on three field goals your team gained confidence and headed for a fine 9-1 season.

5. Review a list of your graduating seniors making comments on the contributions of each to your program.

6. Comment on your returning players, position changes that might be forthcoming, etc.

7. Explain the next step in your football program. This might be your winter off-season weight program. Describe how it works, what is expected of the players, and what you hope to gain by having it. If you are allowed to have spring practice, comment on your plans such as beginning and ending dates.

8. Complete your season review session with a look at your schedule for next fall. Give dates of the games as well as where each game will be played.

Letter of Thanks to All Who
Contributed to the Football Program

There is always a large group of people who, directly or indirectly, have helped to make your football program a success. Some

of these people are paid, such as your school band director. Others
are not, such as a Booster Club worker. Take time to write a short,
personal letter to each of these people thanking them for their
help during the season. Let each person know that you consider his
contribution important. Here are some people you might consider
writing:

- Booster Club leaders
- Band director (or make the letter directed to all band members)
- Cheerleader sponsor
- Cheerleader captain (or all cheerleaders individually)
- Chain crew
- Stadium or practice field maintenance workers
- Concession stand workers
- Program sellers
- Public address announcer
- Team doctors
- Head of the football officials association
- Game photographers
- School principal or superintendent
- School counselors (who help with college transcripts of those
  players being recruited)
- Newspaper, radio, or TV reporters who have worked with the
  team
- Transportation people
- Parents of players (especially seniors)

The letter need not be long, but should be personal and should
make the person receiving it feel that his efforts in your team's
behalf were appreciated. Follow the example in Figure 11-1.

Send Films of Prospects to Colleges

As soon as your season is over collect your game films from
other schools around your area who have borrowed them. Have
them available to send to colleges that are interested in recruiting
any of your players. Most colleges, whether they have seen your
players perform in person or not, will request film of a player so
that other coaches on the college staff can make an evaluation.

After collecting all of your films take time to sit down and
quickly review each one. Make sure there are no breaks or tears in

November 27, 19____

Dear Mr. _____,
       Just a line to thank you on behalf of the 19____ Central
High Chargers for your contribution to our football program
this fall. Serving as our public address announcer is a job that
requires much time and effort. We annually receive many good
comments on your work and we are glad to have a person of
your capabilities handle this very important task.
       If we can be of service to you, please let us know.

              Sincerely,

              _____ (your signature)

Figure 11-1

---

the film. But most important of all, look for the roll of film which
best shows what each *prospect* can do. As you are watching each
film take notes such as:

> "The second half of the _____ High game shows
> our split end (a college prospect) catching two passes (28 yards
> and a 31 yard TD)."
> "Second half of _____ High game shows our QB
> running the option play well, making a 14 yard TD run, and
> completing 5 dropback passes."
> "The first quarter of the _____ High game
> shows good blocking by our left tackle. We are on offense most
> of the quarter."

Taking notes such as these insures that you are sending the
film that best shows the talents of your split end, QB, and left
tackle to the colleges.

Send Equipment for Renovation

       There are a number of respectable renovating companies in
the country who do good work at a reasonable price. If you choose
to renovate some of your used equipment (some coaches don't)
check with other coaches and get the name of a good company—
one that provides prompt service, good repair work, and reasonable prices.

Be sure the equipment you send is worth repairing. Some repair costs could be almost as high as the cost of *new* equipment. Shoulder pads, helmets, and shoes are the items that most coaches consider renovating.

If you contract with a company to renovate your equipment, be sure to get an estimate of the costs and also find out how long it will take to do the work. If you have spring practice you will need the equipment back before the starting date of practice.

Make Initial Plans for the Off-season Conditioning Program

By our definition, an off-season conditioning program is run from two to five days a week (after school hours), involves next fall's football prospects, and is operated by all football coaches not involved with winter sports such as basketball or wrestling. The program involves agility drills, running, stretching exercises, and weight training.

We like to start the program about three weeks after the end of the football season (this would be early December), although we sometimes wait until school starts back after Christmas holidays.

Our two aims in the off-season program are to develop more strength and agility in the football players who will return to play for us next fall, and to find some new athletes who haven't been in our program before.

The first step is to ask your principal to allow you to meet with *all* 9th, 10th, and 11th grade boys in your school. This meeting should be in late November or early December, several weeks after your last football game. With the permission of the principal, hold the meeting during school hours (either the first thing in the morning or the last thing in the afternoon). This is the only way you can be assured of speaking to every boy in school. Hold the meeting in the auditorium, gym, or cafeteria. Make the meeting short and to the point. Tell the boys that you and your staff are starting next fall's football program *now*. All of them are invited to take part provided they are willing to work. Tell them that if they plan to play they must start now by getting involved in your off-season program. This allows newcomers to work into the football program slowly, and gives the coaches a chance to determine who wants to work and who doesn't. After the brief meeting ask any boy who wants to play next fall (including your returning players) to come to you and get an information sheet, fill it out and return it to you within one week. Figure 11-2 shows a sample off-season workout and conditioning program information sheet.

OFF-SEASON CONDITIONING PROGRAM
INFORMATION SHEET

Name _____Present grade _____

Address _____Phone No. _____

Parent's name _____Business Phone _____

Father's occupation _____Mother's Occupation _____

Your age as of Dec. 1, 19____ is _____ Birthday: _____

Check one: _____ I am presently playing basketball for our school and will not be able to be in the off-season program, but want to play football.

_____ I am presently wrestling for our school and will not be able to be in the off-season program, but want to play football.

_____ I want to play football and will begin the off-season conditioning program now.

Put a No. 1 by your first choice of an offensive position. Put a No. 2 by your second choice and a No. 3 by your 3rd choice:

_____ QB _____ Running back _____ Split end

_____ Tight end _____ Center _____ Guard _____ Tackle

Put a No. 1, 2, or 3 by your first three choices of a defensive position:

_____ Defensive back _____ Linebacker

_____ Defensive end _____ Defensive lineman

List your approximate size: Height: _____ Weight: _____

Have you had any weight-lifting experience? _____

If so, where? _____

Please return this information sheet to Coach _____

before December _____ .

Your parent's signature here indicates his(her) approval of your joining our football off-season conditioning program.

Parent's signature _____

Figure 11-2

As each player returns the completed form give him a mimeographed sheet (see example in Figure 11-3) which will provide dates, times, and general workout information (page 170).

Pay Officials, Photographer, Laundry, etc.

Many of the people who worked for you during the season—your photographer, the laundry man, game officials—may not have been paid on a game-to-game basis. Check carefully with your

CENTRAL CHARGERS
OFF-SEASON FOOTBALL PROGRAM

We will start ....Monday, December _____ 19____
We will end this program ....at the start of spring practice
  (Note: if you have no spring practice, you might wish the program to
  continue until May)
If you are . . . a varsity lineman, work out every Monday, Wednesday, and
  Friday from 3:00 p.m. until 4:30 p.m.
      . . . a varsity back or receiver, work out every Tuesday, Thursday,
  and Friday from 3:00 p.m. until 4:30 p.m.
      . . . a JV (or new to the program) lineman, work out every Monday
  and Wednesday from 4:30 p.m. until 5:30 p.m.
      . . . a JV (or new to the program) back or receiver, work out every
  Tuesday and Thursday from 4:30 p.m. until 5:30 p.m.
Equipment: Bring your own. Wear only orange or white (school colors)
  T-shirts and shorts. White socks only. Tennis shoes.
  (Notice: for team organization, discipline, and morale you will not be allowed to work out in jeans, street shoes, etc.)
Dressing Room: The varsity dressing room will be open 15 minutes before
  and after workouts. Use the lockers on a day-to-day basis. Do not
  leave any equipment in a locker.
Workout excuse: If you are sick, you *must* call the coaches' office and let the
  coach know that you won't be in due to illness. Failure to inform the
  coach may cause you to be dropped from the team. The coaches' office phone number is _____ .

The workouts will be organized. Report to the dressing room on time and
change clothes quickly. Line up outside the weight room. Do not start on any
exercise or drill until instructed by the coach. Move quickly from one drill or
weight to another on the coach's command. Keep noise to a minimum!

Figure 11-3

---

business manager concerning these people. Review how often they were used and the price that was agreed upon before the season. Get their checks in the mail as soon as possible with a note of thanks for their good service.

Remove Sled Pads, Store Dummys, Chains, etc.

Don't neglect to take the pads off your two-man and your seven-man sleds. Coaches sometimes forget to do this after the last practice, if the practice field is not clearly in view from the main school buildings.

Clean the pads, your air dummys, the chains and down marker. Store these items in a safe, dry place. Make a note of needed repairs or replacements.

Speaking Engagement Schedule

After the season is over your speaking schedule may actually be more demanding than ever (especially if you had a good season). (See *Speaking Engagement Schedule*—Chapter 9—September.) Continue to keep an accurate record of your future speaking engagements.

Remember to get the following information from any person or group that asks you to speak:

- Date and time
- Location
- Type of people in attendance (parents? young people? a mixture of both? men only? women only?)
- Type of speech desired (humorous? serious? inspirational?)
- Length of speech
- Dress (formal or informal)

Save Final Records, Stats, etc. on Teams Around the State

Whether or not you already know what teams you will play next fall, begin collecting records, stats, etc. on teams around the state. There are at least three ways this can be done:

- Watch newspapers for final stats on a certain team, or more important, a certain league or region.
- Talk with other coaches who have access to records and stats from around the state.
- Write the league statisticians of leagues around the state requesting a copy of their stats (send a self-addressed, stamped envelope).

Once gathered, file these statistics under one of two headings:

- Teams that you will probably play during your regular schedule
- Possible playoff opponents

Then, as you meet a team next fall, refer to these statistics. Hopefully, you will pick up a clue that can give you an edge. To use the stats:

1. Scratch out the names of seniors who have graduated.

2. Note returning players. Look carefully at what each player accomplished. For example, you may notice that one returning back carried the football 44 times but had no run longer than 7 yards. This could indicate the back is not the breakaway type.

3. Look for offensive trends. Statistics may show that of the 62 passes that were caught, split ends caught 55, while the tight end caught only 5 and the running backs caught only 2. Indication here is that the offense is split-end oriented when it comes to passing.

4. Look for team weaknesses. You may discover that one opponent was ranked No. 2 in a 10-team league in rushing defense, but that they were dead last in pass defense. Another team may have good stats in all areas except the kicking game where their punter (who returns) averaged only 28.3 a punt and had 5 kicks blocked. This could be your key to defeating this team.

Save the statistics from year to year and you may see patterns developing. Some team may, year after year, seem to gain most of its yardage on short runs while another seems to gain most of its yardage on occasionally completed long passes.

Take Down Old Bulletin Board Material

Throughout the long season just completed, your bulletin board probably collected a great deal of material. Some of it should now be thrown away. Items announcing the time for the last pre-game meal, the date that equipment is to be turned in, or what color jersey we will wear in our last home game, are no longer of importance.

Some articles, however, should be saved:

Inspirational articles . . . file these away in your desk . . . they can be used again another season.

Scouting reports . . . save and use when you play these same teams next fall.

Photographs . . . if they are of your players, file them for future use or give them to the players . . . do the same with photos of the cheerleaders . . . save any photos of opposing players (taken from opponent's program) especially if the photos are of players who return next fall . . . if the photos are of game action (possibly taken by a newspaper photographer), frame them and hang them in your locker room.

Football-related cartoons . . . save for future use.

In the past few weeks your players have probably looked at

the bulletin board several times, but upon seeing "the same material" on it have neglected to read it. Now that you have taken down all the old material, you have an excellent opportunity to get across new points with an attractive new bulletin board featuring fresh material.

Put up things like:

- Next fall's schedule
- Changes in next fall's uniforms
- Names of newly elected cheerleaders (the election may not take place until later in the year)
- Next fall's Homecoming date
- Football banquet date and time, as well as the name of the banquet speaker
- The date football letters, jackets, and/or sweaters are expected to arrive
- Information concerning off-season workouts

Repair Sled Pads, Dummys, etc.

Last month you should have taken sled pads off the sleds and stored your dummys. If any of these items needed repairing, you should have sent them to the renovator by now. Time is especially important if your school is allowed to have spring practice and you plan to start in late February or March.

Clean and Store Footballs

This may be one of the most neglected items on your post season checklist. It is quite natural, after the final game, to throw the footballs in a bag and then throw the bag in a corner of the locker room or equipment room.

If you haven't cleaned them yet, follow these steps:

1. Take all footballs from the bag and spread them out so they can dry thoroughly (especially if the last practices or the last game were played in the rain).

2. Take a rag or a brush (one that is not too stiff) and clean the dirt from each ball.

3. Clean the ball with a commercial ball-cleaning product (several brands are available).

4. Deflate the football.

5. Separate the footballs into groups . . . several could be used next fall as game balls . . . others will make excellent practice balls for the varsity . . . some can be passed down to the JV team . . . a few may need to be discarded.

6. Store the balls in a safe, dry place.

Check Insurance Claims to Be Sure All Have Been Sent In

Regardless of the type football insurance policy your team had this season you, as coach, probably had to send in claim forms to the insurance company each time a player was injured. You probably have done this already. But a final check is important. Failure to send in a claim within a certain time period will make the claim void.

Here are some steps to follow to help you in this checkup:

1. Make a list of every player you can think of who was injured and needed medical care this past season. Ask your coaches to review the list and make additions, if any. Ask players whom you see each day to help compile this list (or hold a team meeting for this purpose if needed).

2. Talk personally with each player who was injured and ask if he received prompt medical payment for the injury.

3. In some cases it might be necessary to contact the parents of the injured player to determine if medical payment has been taken care of properly.

4. If you find a player who was injured, but no claim form was turned in to the insurance company, sit down with him immediately and fill out the claim forms. If you feel that the deadline date for filing the claim is very near you might need to make a personal call to the insurance company explaining that the claim is being sent immediately.

By all means don't neglect this important duty. Your school might end up having to pay the bill out of your athletic account.

Decide Spring Practice Dates

If your school is allowed to hold several weeks of spring football practice (some states allow this and others don't), you need to go ahead and decide your spring practice dates. Most teams in warmer weather states like to hold spring practice in late February and March. Some teams prefer having these workouts in May, near the end of the school year. Here are some factors that you need to consider as you plan your dates:

If you plan your practice in *late February*, . . . will your basketball season be over by this time? will the basketball season likely be extended by tournament play? are any of your key football players involved with basketball? will any football players still be involved in wrestling? will spring practice be over in time to prepare for the baseball and track seasons? what type weather can be expected this time of the year? will your school's spring holidays be in March and interfere with spring practice? will you have four weeks of practice or can you cut it down to three weeks and still get in all of your work?

If you plan your practice in *May* . .. will the baseball and track seasons be over? how many football players are involved with baseball or track? will either of these teams likely be involved in post-season games or meets? will other school activities (dances, year end meetings, etc.) interfere with your spring practice schedule? what type of weather can be counted on at this time of the year?

Once your decision has been made put the dates on the school calendar. Inform your coaches and players of the dates. Send the information to the local media.

Make List of All Equipment Needs
for Spring Practice

Chances are that you purchased plenty of equipment for the season just completed, and this same equipment will be in good shape for spring practice (some states allow several weeks of spring practice). However, you may have a larger turnout of players for spring practice than you had in the fall (you should if your program is growing); therefore, you need to take stock of the usable equipment on hand. As long as the equipment is safe, spring practice equipment doesn't have to be new.

Check briefly to see what major items will be needed. You probably already have a good idea that you are short on some items, such as knee pads, tape, or medical supplies. List these items, taking into consideration how many people you are expecting out for spring practice. Ideally, you would like to have every player dressed and ready to go the first day of spring practice. But since this is a more informal time, you may prefer not to purchase extra equipment now, but wait, instead, to see exactly what you need when practice starts. If you run a little short of equipment, you may consider letting your senior lettermen work in shorts or sweats the first week until you can pick up the extra equipment you need. Remember, in spring practice you will not need equipment that must be ordered months in advance. Pants, jerseys, hip pads, shoes, shoulder pads, and even helmets can be picked up (or delivered to your school) from some sporting goods company in the area within a few days.

Inventory All Football-Related Equipment

This needs to be done at least twice during the year in order to know exactly where you stand with equipment.

Purchase a small notebook. With the aid of a fellow coach, your equipment manager, or a student manager count each piece of football-related equipment. Note its condition, and record the information in the notebook. Have a page for each item as shown in Figure 12-1.

FOOTBALL INVENTORY

Item ....Helmets
Date ....December—1982
Number usable 95
Condition ....Excellent 35　Good　25　Average 21　Fair 9　Poor 5
Added ....10 new, February, 1983
Discarded ....5 poor, February 1983
Item ....Helmets
Date ....June—1983
Number usable 100
Condition ....Excellent 45　Good 25　Average 21　Fair 9　Poor 0

Figure 12-1

(*Note:* keep this type of chart up-to-date as you make twice-a-year inventories.)

Have a separate page for each of the following items:

- helmets
- chin straps

- shoulder pads
- hip pads
- knee pads
- thigh pads
- shoes
- socks
- supporters
- footballs
- kicking tees
- practice jerseys
- game jerseys
- game pants
- belts
- travel bags
- practice pants
- wrist bands
- towels
- cases of tape
- shoestrings
- shoulder pad straps
- game shoes
- dummys
- set of chains
- down marker
- sled pads
- projector
- camera (for filming game)
- medical kit (equipped)

Sign Up Prospects for Spring Practice, or for Next Fall

If you are having an off-season conditioning program you have already done this (see Chapter 11—November). Whether you have spring practice or will not practice again until the fall, you should begin recruiting your players now for next season. You simply can't wait until summer to try to contact those interested in playing in the fall. You need time to *know* your players, to follow their school grades and conduct, and to mold them into athletes ready to be coached in the spring or fall.

Meet with all boys in school (except graduating seniors, of course). Have them sign information sheets, or at least get the names of those interested in playing. Throughout the remainder of the school year watch and work with them. When practice starts, you will know something about the characteristics and attitudes of each boy.

Begin Off-season Conditioning Program

Re-read *Make initial plans for off-season conditioning program* as described in Chapter 11—November. If you plan to have such a program, you need to start now, or at least in January.

Make sure your weight room and other workout areas are clean and free from any unnecessary clutter. Be sure you and your coaches have organized yourselves well and are prepared to present a first-class program for your players. Each coach should have a definite part of the workout program to control.

Some of you may wish to work entirely on weights. Others may concentrate on running and agility. Many will want to combine the best features of both.

Review Budget and Adjust According to Football Gate Receipts

Read again the section in Chapter 6—June, headed *Plan Budget for the Coming School Year*. After doing this take a careful look at the gate receipts from the just-completed season. There are three directions you can take:

1. If your gate receipts from football are about what you expected, leave your athletic budget as it is.

2. If you had a good season at the gate and made more money than anticipated, you can (a) save the extra money for emergencies or put it in a savings account, or (b) you can increase the budget of each sport. For example, if you made 10% more money than anticipated, you can increase football, basketball, track, baseball, golf, and tennis budgets by 10% each.

3. If you did not do as well at the gate as you had expected, you will need to cut each sport's budget. For example, if your gate receipts were 5% below your June estimate, you need to cut the budget of all sports by 5%.

(You will need to take another look at your budget immediately after the *basketball* season and adjust each sport's budget according to the profit or loss figures.)

Ask TD Club for Football Camp Financial Commitment

If you plan to take your team to a week of concentrated work out of town (football camp) next fall, now is the time to think about the finances.

Contact the president of your TD Club and review with him your plans for camp. Explain how much money you will need and ask the club's assistance in raising some of it. Be careful not to "ask for a handout." Tell him your players will be willing to work on any projects necessary to help raise money. Explain that preparing for camp is a long process and that as soon as possible you will need the total amount of money the club can provide for you. This will go a long way in determining how many players you will be able to take to camp.

Prepare Press Releases for College Football Signees

If you have any senior players who will sign with *major universities*, they will be given ample press coverage. However, if one or more of your players sign with some of the smaller colleges, you will need to provide information to the local media. Some small colleges don't have the funds to promote their signees, but you can get your deserving players recognition if you work at it.

First, wait until the player has been offered financial aid to play football and has made his decision to attend a particular school. Talk with a representative of the school and find out the date, time, and place of the signing. Call members of the local press nad request that they attend the signing, take a picture (newspaper), and get a few quotes from the player and the coach who handles the signing.

The signing can take place at the player's home or perhaps in the school (library, principal's office). If possible mimeograph a short reminder of the player's accomplishments and hand these out to the press representatives. This will aid them in preparing their story.

If a press representative (from the newspaper, radio, or television) can't be present, type a short summary of the signing and send it to the reporter who handles high school football.

Order Jackets and Letters

The season has been over several weeks and players who will be awarded letters (and jackets or sweaters if this is your school policy) have been selected (see Chapter 11—November).

Order your letters and jackets as early as possible. If they are special order, they will take several weeks to receive. If a local dealer has these items in stock, you should be able to get them in a few days.

If possible, have the letters and jackets ready to present the night of your football banquet.

Secure Bids for Helmets, Game Pants, and Game Jerseys

You cannot order special jerseys and game pants in your team colors and designs too soon. We suggest they be ordered next month (see Chapter 1—January). To do this you need to get bids on these two items, along with helmets (your team color with your style of face mask attached), right away.

First, decide exactly what you want in game equipment. (Will you keep your jerseys and pants the same as last fall?) Write out a complete description of what you want, complete with sizes, colors, etc. Contact all sporting goods dealers in your area and ask if they want to bid on these items. You may want the bids to be separate on each item (pants-helmet-jersey). Or you may prefer a total bid on all three items (make this clear to the dealers). Tell the dealers that the order will go to the dealer with the lowest bid *as long as he can guarantee a reasonable delivery date*. (If ordered in January, the goods should be in by the end of May or early June at the latest. If a dealer can't guarantee this, you may wish to pass on his bid. You can't afford to be worrying in late July or August when your game equipment is arriving.)

Give the dealers a definite time to bring in their bids (one week is usually long enough). To be safe, you might want to open the bids in the presence of your principal (to keep from being accused of playing a favorite dealer).

Immediately inform all dealers who submitted a bid of the results. (You don't have to tell a dealer how close he was in the bidding, simply tell one that he had the lowest bid and tell the others that they were not low bid, but you appreciate their cooperation.)

Check any Unpaid Bills Relating to Football

Before closing the books on football, review with your principal and business manager all bills relating to football. By December all, or most, should have been paid. Try to avoid a delay in paying bills. If there is a reason why someone or some company has not been paid you might want to drop them a note of explanation.

Final Junior Varsity Rating Sheet

As the varsity coach you cannot always observe all of your *Junior Varsity* players in every situation. Chances are that you have seen them play, and perhaps worked with some of them yourself, but still you don't know them as your JV coaches do. These are your future varsity players and you need to know everything possible about them. Some may be ready to move up to the varsity and others need another year on the JV team.

Ask your JV coaches to give you a complete report on each player. This can be done in two ways:

1. Ask your JV coaches to list each player who came out during the season on a *checklist rating sheet* (see Figure 12-2). This will give you a *brief*, but very important, picture of each player.

JV PLAYER CHECKLIST RATING SHEET

Key: 5= great   4=good   3=average   2=fair   1=poor

Player	Off. Pos.	Def. Pos.	Attitude	Hustle	Size
Lee Olson	End	LB	5	5	3

Speed	Football Ability	Toughness	Practice Attendance
4	4	4	5

Intelligence	Varsity Potential
4	4

Figure 12-2

2. Besides the checklist rating sheet, we ask the JV coaches to write a *brief paragraph* giving their thoughts about each player. Include here any bit of information that would help the varsity coach make a final evaluation of the player's football future on the varsity. Figure 12-3 shows some sample paragraphs.

Lee Olson . . . this young player is a real asset to our football program. He works hard in the off-season to improve himself. He started at tight end and played linebacker when things got tough. Is not one of our bigger players but has great heart. Could be varsity starter next fall!

Bob Lowery . . . has great size (6-4, 208), but was a disappointment to us. Practice attendance was not good. Only a fair "hitter" despite being the largest player on JV team. Has not shown real interest in football. Is worth talking to this winter—may come around and help if attitude changes. School grades a problem.

Tom Birch . . . good size and speed. Our leading scorer though he was hurt (broken hand) early in the season. May be a better split end than halfback. Excellent pass receiver.

Ken Hall . . . small, tough, and determined. Don't know where to recommend playing him, but play him somewhere. Overlook lack of size . . . he's a winner!!!

Figure 12-3

Index